D0850501

AMERICAN ART SONG
and
AMERICAN POETRY

Volume I:
America Comes of Age

Ruth C. Friedberg

The Scarecrow Press, Inc.
Metuchen, N.J., & London
1981

Library of Congress Cataloging in Publication Data

Friedberg, Ruth C., 1928-
    American art song and American poetry.

    Includes bibliographies and indexes.
    Contents: v. 1. America comes of age.
    1. Songs, English--United States--History
and criticism.   I. Title.
ML2811.F75   784.3'00973   81-9047
ISBN 0-8108-1460-9   AACR2

To S. J. F.

CONTENTS

FOREWORD

Little has been written about the American art song and even less about settings of specifically American poetry. As a partial remedy, I have undertaken a series of studies in several volumes that will treat selected American songs of the past hundred years, from MacDowell to the present. My focus has at all times been the interrelationships between the composer and the poet, and the ways in which these have influenced the completed song. I have tried to select pieces that are not only important contributions to the performing literature but that also illuminate some phase of America's cultural past.

One of the advantages of studying relatively recent musical literature is that many of its composers are still alive. In the effort to gain firsthand knowledge of their own views on American art songs, I have exchanged many letters and conducted a number of interviews with American song composers whenever time, funding, and geography would permit. I intend to continue and expand this type of personal contact while gathering material for the remaining volumes of this series. It should also be mentioned that such composers as Persichetti, Nordoff, Rorem, and Duke, whose comments on American poetry and the processes of word setting are quoted in the introductory chapters of this book, will reappear in subsequent volumes in which their own songs will be treated.

Volume II, to be titled Voices of Maturity, will begin with Mary Howe's settings of Elinor Wylie and Virgil Thomson's of Marianne Moore. Some of the other composers projected for inclusion are John Duke, Charles Naginski, Howard Swanson, Paul Bowles, David Diamond, Samuel Barber and Vincent Persichetti along with such poetic counterparts as e. e. cummings, E. A. Robinson, Sara Teasdale, Tennessee Williams, Herman Melville, and James Agee. The working title of Volume III is The Century Advances. As the title suggests, this volume will deal not only with long-established composers of the stature of Ned Rorem but also with William Flanagan and some younger and more recently recognized figures, such as Robert Baksa, Gerald Ginsburg, Thomas Pasatieri, and John Corigliano, Jr. Representative of the poets to be discussed in Volume III are Stephen Crane, Wallace Stevens, Edward Albee, Howard Moss, and William Hoffman.

Throughout these studies, the term "art song" will be used to refer only to settings of already-existent poetry, thus excluding folksongs. Moreover, the word "song" will be used only in the sense of solo song with piano accompaniment, so that compositions for more than one voice or for voice and chamber group will not be discussed.

Although I expect that my audience will be primarily musicians, it is my hope that it will also include lovers of poetry and many of those engaged in the study of various facets of American civilization. It is my further hope that sufficient interest will be generated in a number of fine settings that are now out of print (as indicated in the notes) to encourage their reissuing.

I should like to thank John Hanks, professor of voice at Duke University, for introducing me to the American art song literature, and composers Ian Hamilton and Gerard Jaffe for their suggestions on the scope and direction of this work. My thanks also to Patricia Goodson and Janann Stark for their assistance in preparing this manuscript for publication.

Ruth C. Friedberg

AMERICAN ART SONG AND AMERICAN POETRY
Volume I: America Comes of Age

PROLOGUE

At the conclusion of his illuminating article "Problems of a
Song-Writer," Mario Castelnuovo-Tedesco made the following
generous and provocative statement in 1944: "... let me
express a hope that English-speaking people (Americans es-
pecially) find in their admirable poetry--which has given so
much joy to me, an Italian, a rich source of inspiration for
their song literature, towards the furthering of happiness
and fraternity among men, as their great poet Whitman
would have wished. "[1]

Leaving aside this composer's noble but perhaps un-
realistic trust in the salvation of humankind through the art
song, we may still find in his statement three suggestions
of the greatest importance to the present study. The first,
which is not new but which receives expressive emphasis
here, is the widespread ardor of Western civilization for
English-language poetry. The second is the crucial dis-
tinction that is made between American poetry and that of
other English-speaking peoples. The third is the implica-
tion, fortunately less common today than it was thirty years
ago, that Americans have indeed not already produced a
large body of song literature based on this very source of
inspiration.

The American art song has, in fact, profited great-
ly from the general explosion of interest in American music
that was attendant on the Bicentennial celebrations. The
past decade has brought forth a plethora of recordings,
books, articles, bibliographies, and performances center-
ing on the existent literature, as well as a number of com-

missions and incentives for new compositions in this genre. Although only recently beginning to be afforded full recognition, the American art song is not a new phenomenon, having developed over the last hundred years with literature worthy of note in all periods of its chronology. One of its problems, which can also be seen as a source of strength, has been America's possession of a common language with another civilization--admittedly an ancestor of our own, but a civilization that no longer entirely represents us. This situation has in the past produced the kind of cultural schizophrenia that characterized much of American artistic thinking: the need to escape from, to rebel against, to go beyond or outside of the British and European heritage, mingled strongly with the desire to learn from, to emulate, and to draw the water of life out of this same fountainhead. "We are transposed Europeans, " said Paul Nordoff, "and have been robbed of our heritage. "[2] Vincent Persichetti, on the other hand, has seen in the American nature the well-developed and desirable talent of "taking a little from everyone" to create a sort of "one-world" synthesis. [3]

Regardless of one's stance toward the relationship of America's culture and particularly of its language to the countries of origin, our situation vis-à-vis the art song remains unique. Whereas one is confronted with the proper and satisfying spectacle of German composers setting German poets and French composers setting French poets (among the rare exceptions are Hugo Wolf's Italian and Spanish songbooks), the American composer seeking a text has always had the problem of choosing between William Blake or Walt Whitman, A. E. Housman or Emily Dickinson, W. B. Yeats or Robert Frost, and an infinite number of similar British or American possibilities. This writer maintains that a particular aesthetic strength emerges from the cultural reinforcement of American composers setting the works of American poets, and it is to the consideration of selected examples of such collaborations that these studies are dedicated.

*   *   *

A brief consideration of the roots of American poetry and song seems in order here. In her excellent treatment of the ancestors of American art song, Grace Yerbury confesses, "All my life I wished to find America

4

original in the arts.   I know now she has not been. "[4]
Given America's beginnings as a colony, an initially de-
rivative culture would hardly seem surprising.   Indeed,
"influences" on creative artists have often proved to be en-
riching contributions to their personal stylistic syntheses.
The great J. S. Bach himself is generally recognized as
having combined German, French, and Italian elements in
his ultimately universal style.   It is nevertheless the au-
thor's contention that America does eventually find her own
voice both in poetry and in song and that this finding has
its beginnings in the nineteenth century and its flowering in
the twentieth.   Nor are we lacking in "breakthrough" fig-
ures, artists who do not merely reflect their age but who
create a new one through basic changes in the language of
their art form.   Few would deny that Walt Whitman and
Emily Dickinson hold such a place in literature, as does
Charles Ives in music.

In order to trace the rise of any song tradition, we
must begin with the poetry, for it is a fact well known to
music historians that the great ages of song composition in
all countries always follow, with a variable time lag, the
great periods of lyric poetry.   The golden age of German
lieder trails on the heels of Germany's poetic outpourings
of early Romanticism.   French song comes into its own in
the late nineteenth century upon inspiration from Verlaine
and the Symbolists.   In America, the sequence of events is
the same, but her poetry develops very slowly in colonial
times.   The earliest forms are funeral verses and reli-
gious meditations, for the Puritans allowed little range to
the arts except where they might directly serve the sober
purposes of life in this world and contemplation of the
world to come.   Interestingly enough, this metaphysical
stance, this search for personal meaning in a world full of
darkness and evil, becomes one of, if not the dominating
theme of the entire history of American poetry.

With the passing of Puritanism, the coming of the
Enlightenment and all the upheavals attendant on the Amer-
ican Revolution eventually produced the new social, po-
litical, and cultural climate of the early nineteenth century.
The times were now ripening for America's authentic lit-
erary voice to emerge.   Longfellow, Whittier, Bryant,
Lowell, and Holmes are the first to consider themselves
"poets" by principal profession, [5] thus publicly declaring the
importance to our civilization of the poetic art, but their

writings are still largely derivative. It remains for Walt Whitman at mid-century to strike out in new directions and draw universal attention to the now fully matured artistic creativity of America.

* * *

The early history of song and singing in this country begins, as we would expect, in the same place as its poetry, with the liturgical needs of the Puritans, Moravians, Hermits of Wissahickon, [6] and other persuasions. At the same time, a strong secular tradition produces battle and marching songs, and, particularly in the eighteenth century, many ballad operas and various "parody" forms, all of which are based on British or continental models.

In the first half of the nineteenth century, American song is dominated by the sentimental ballad, also an English derivation, which in time shows variation in form, melody, and harmony stemming from French and Italian sources. [7] Born half a century later than the "Longfellow school" of poets, Edward MacDowell stands in an analogous position to them in music, as the first to achieve recognition as a valid American composer, although his language never really breaks away from his German training. Once again, it remains for a renegade, this time Charles Ives, to find fresh pathways.

* * *

This volume will begin with an overview of how American composers and poets have approached some of the basic problems of word setting. It will then deal with selected song literature of the late nineteenth and early twentieth centuries. This was the crucial period for art song in the United States, as it pushed toward the light of day from European roots but through American soil, and emerged as an unmistakable flower of the New World. We shall see MacDowell, Loeffler, and Griffes setting the largely Romantic poetry of nineteenth-century America in an amalgam of German and French musical styles. Then we shall see Charles Ives, the iconoclast, setting eleven American poets and using his songs as a medium in which to develop the new modes of musical expression that were his continuing concern. And, finally, we shall encounter a group of composers, setting poetry from Emily Dickinson to Theodore

Roethke, who became firmly established in the judgment of the world community as "American" and who labored consciously to express their native culture in a musical language that derived from it, in both character and content.

NOTES

1. Mario Castelnuovo-Tedesco, "Music and Poetry: Problems of a Songwriter, " in Reflections on Art, ed. Susanne Langer (Baltimore: Johns Hopkins Press, 1958), p. 310. This article originally appeared in The Musical Quarterly, vol. 30, no. 1 (1944), pp. 102-111.

2. The late American composer Paul Nordoff, in an interview with the author at the home of Mrs. Curtis Bok, Philadelphia, Pennsylvania, February 5, 1975.

3. Vincent Persichetti, in an interview with the author at Theodore Presser Co. , Bryn Mawr, Pennsylvania, February 3, 1975.

4. Grace D. Yerbury, Song in America from Early Times to About 1850 (Metuchen, New Jersey: Scarecrow Press, 1971), p. iv.

5. Hyatt H. Waggoner, American Poets from the Puritans to the Present (New York: Dell, 1968), p. 34.

6. The Hermits of Wissahickon, a little-known mystic sect of German origin, is described by Yerbury, p. 37.

7. This statement summarizes the detailed and thorough treatment of the early nineteenth-century American ballad found in Yerbury, Part II.

I. THE AMERICAN APPROACH TO WORD-SETTING

Robert Schumann described the desirable relationship between text and setting in these words: "The poem should lie like a bride in the minstrel's arm, free, happy, and entire."[1] American composers of today feel the same passion for the poetry they set. "I love our language," Paul Nordoff said, "and it's very good for poetry. This is because the large number of one syllable words make it flexible and adaptable to many rhythms, and also because of the great number of similar words which have slightly different meanings."[2] Vincent Persichetti reads a great deal of poetry and prefers it to newspapers or novels. He may realize only after considerable passage of time that he wants to set a particular poem to music.[3]

Several of our song composers, notably Edward Mac-Dowell and Charles Ives, have been sufficiently moved by the poetic impulse to set their own texts. Indeed, Mac-Dowell was convinced that language and music could be most effectively combined only if the same person had written both. Ned Rorem takes strong exception to this point of view. "The most important thing," he maintains, "is that what a composer sets is good poetry. I don't set my own poetry because I don't think it's good literature." He also feels that attempts at writing poetry with the avowed purpose of setting it to music are doomed to failure.[4]

In the face of so much devotion professed by composers to the art of poetry, it is curious to observe Calvin S. Brown's statement in Music and Literature that "remarkably little attention has been given to the relationship

between text and music. "[5] Perhaps if comparison is made
with the total weight of musical aesthetic studies in existence,
this charge may prove well founded, but it is also true that
for the past hundred years a considerable body of writing on
this very relationship has emerged from the composers, poets,
critics, and aestheticians of this country. There are three
main areas into which most of the problems of word setting seem
to fall in these discussions. The first has to do with pros-
ody, and all rhythmic aspects of the poetry and musical set-
ting, both separately and together. The second involves tone
color--the "pure sound" component, we might say--which also
has an ostensibly different meaning in verse than it has in
music. The third area, the most difficult in some ways, is
that of word meaning. Here the battle continues between
those who believe, as did Stravinsky, that music, unlike words,
cannot "express" anything, and those who attempt to prove,
often by involved systematic analysis, that it can and does.

A composer beginning to deal with the first problem
area, that of the rhythmic scheme for a setting, is at once
faced with the necessity of deciding whether or not to em-
ploy what Donald Ivey, in his illuminating study on Song,
calls a "literal transfer of poetic meter to musical."[6] An
example of this from the American song repertoire would be
John Duke's setting of e. e. cummings's "The Mountains
Are Dancing, " which begins:

When / fa - ces called / flow - ers float / out of the / ground
And / breath - ing is / wish - ing and / wish - ing is / having

Duke has exactly paralleled the strong dactylic pattern with
a 3/8 meter that has a corresponding "swing" and accent
distribution.

Example 1.1, measures 8-16. "The Mountains Are Dancing, "
by John Duke. Copyright © 1956 by Carl Fischer, Inc. New
York. International Copyright Secured. All Rights Reserved.
Reprinted by permission of the Publisher.

9

If the composer decides against the literal transfer, he or she is then free to choose a rhythmic scheme that stems from widely varying factors of word sound or meaning. Aaron Copland, for instance, in "The Chariot" (the last of his Twelve Poems of Emily Dickinson), is setting a clear iambic meter:

Be - cause / I would / not stop / for Death
He kind / - ly stopped / for me.
The car - / riage held / but just / our - selves
And Im - / mor - tal / - i - ty.

Sensing no doubt that a literal transfer was not appropriate here, the composer instead chose a subtle rhythmic scheme in which the dotted patterns suggest the motion of the carriage, and the long-held tones, the pause in the rush of living imposed by Death's visit.

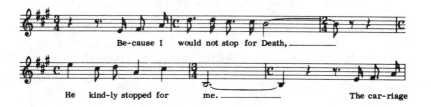

Example 1. 2, measures 6-11.   Copyright © 1951 by Aaron Copland; renewed 1979.   Reprinted by permission of Aaron Copland, copyright owner, and Boosey & Hawkes, Inc., sole licensee.

When the process of transfer just described is treated by critics and scholars, one finds, perhaps not too surprisingly, that while some are prone to stress the differences between musical and poetic rhythm, others go to considerable lengths to stress their similarity.   In an intriguing little book called The Science of English Verse, the poet Sidney Lanier, who often brought his years as a professional musician to bear on his creation of and theorizing about poetry, presents the following notion:

> The English habit of uttering words, prose or verse, is to give each sound of each word a duration which

10

is either equal or simply proportionate to the dura-
tion of each other sound; and since these simple
proportions enable the ear to make those exact co-
ordinations of duration which result in the percep-
tion of primary rhythm, we may say that all Eng-
lish word-sounds are primarily rhythmical, and
therefore that the signs of these sounds ... are in
reality also signs of primary rhythm; so that we
may say further, written or printed English words
constitute a sort of system of notation for primary
rhythm. [7]

He goes on to derive secondary rhythms, which approximate
grouping of verse sounds into bars and accents.

Although Lanier's attempt to equate exactly the poetic
foot with the musical measure may seem a bit simplistic
(Calvin S. Brown discusses at some length the reasons for
the greater complexity of musical rhythm), [8] the impulse
stems from the constant pursuit of a kind of rhythmic os-
mosis between words and music that composers and often
poets, too, seem to long for.   John Duke describes his own
version of the pursuit in this way:

I now make a regular practice of making a "rhyth-
mic sketch" or planning out of the time values of
a melody in accordance with my feeling for the
natural rhythmic utterance of the words before I
attempt to conceive the melody as definite pitch
variations.   Of course, this is no good if it does
not become part of a really good melody but (as-
suming that the melody is good) it does make sure
that the words will reinforce and become part of
the whole melodic conception rather than seem to
run counter to the melody as I think they often do
in unconvincing songs. [9]

All aspects of rhythm in word setting must of course
finally come under the larger heading of poetic form.   One
problem that every composer must face is that repetition is
almost a basic principle of musical form, whereas it is fre-
quently destructive in the poetic context.   Ivey discusses in-
stances of text repetition at length, pointing out that deletion
(of entire stanzas or words within a stanza) can be equally
mutilating. [10]   Interestingly, Edward MacDowell, despite his
strong poetic bent and his expressed belief that "song-writing

should follow declamation,"[11] was known on occasion not only to sacrifice natural word accent to melodic design, but to give way (if indeed it is a capitulation) to both word repetition and stanza deletion in the Howells settings we shall discuss in Chapter II.

In the final analysis, it becomes clear that no matter how careful the composer's attention to prosody and poetic form, the musical rhythm will either swallow the poetic feet and stanzas whole or digest them into a new synthesis. The reader should be forewarned that this idea of synthesis will return like a principal theme as we examine the other two problem areas of word setting.

"Tone color," unlike rhythm, is a term that is traditionally familiar in its musical applications but much less so in its poetic meanings. Lawrence Perrins, in Literature-- Structure, Sound, and Sense, points out that poets achieve musical quality by two principal means. One is the arrangement of accents and the other is the choice and arrangement of sounds,[12] which, reduced to the terminology here being employed would read "rhythm" and "tone color." He goes on to indicate that an important factor in sound arrangement is repetition--not repetition of words, which, as already pointed out, must be limited in poetry, but repetition of word components, such as initial consonants (alliteration), final consonants (consonance), vowel sounds (assonance), and combinations of these that can result in rhyme. Poets may use these sound repetitions to create an emphasis (just as they may use the metrical pattern), which leads in turn to the vast possibilities of sound suggesting meaning (onomatopoeia and related usages).

This attribution of the "music" of poetry to the sound arrangements of its syllables and letters appears quite logical. Once again, however, in treating tone color, Sidney Lanier would have us believe that poetry and music present differences in degree rather than in kind, that indeed there are "tunes" in English verse (i. e. , organized melodies of the speaking voice) and that words themselves are musical sounds produced by a reed instrument (the human voice). He goes on to postulate that every vowel, consonant, and combination of letters is a change of tone color and that written letters are therefore a system of notation for tone color (the corollary of his theory of English words as a notational system for rhythm). Finally, he brings in the idea

12

of "scale," which in music represents only selected tones, whereas the scale of verse embraces all possible tones within limits of the human voice. [13]

In looking for the roots of Lanier's remarkable theories, it is not difficult to find them in the writings of Edgar Allan Poe, the idol of his early years. Both men were concerned with the effects of sound and with theories of prosody, and both were interested in the physics of music (Helmholtz in particular influenced Lanier) as well as poetry. In his treatise The Poetic Principle, Poe gives literary expression to these practical concerns. "Music in its various modes of metre, rhythm and rhyme," he says, "is of so vast a moment in Poetry as never to be wisely rejected.... It is in music, perhaps, that the soul most nearly attains the great end for which, when inspired by the Poetic Sentiment, it struggles--the creation of Supernal Beauty." [14] The word "rhyme," it seems clear, was used by Poe to refer to all those aspects of tone color in poetry that we have been discussing.

The question now must arise as to whether these subtle verbal tone colorings of poetry are not also swallowed in song by the more flamboyant timbres of the singing voice and the piano. Certainly, as Donald Ivey points out, composers do on occasion underline poetic alliteration by the use of other musical elements. [15] A good example of this is the following passage from Samuel Barber's "Sure on This Shining Night":

Example 1.3, measures 13-20.   Copyright © 1941 G. Schirmer, Inc.; used by permission.

The initial "h" sounds here are emphasized by both the metrical accent and contour of the melodic line.   But in general it certainly seems true that color factors of poetry, such as alliteration, assonance, and even rhyme, become less important in their own right when absorbed in song and that the concept of a compromise or synthesis of timbres is again useful.

Before we leave our explorations of rhythm and tone color in verse and music, further speculation suggests itself. Some critics seem to feel that the theoretical attempts of Poe and Lanier to equate the music of poetry with the music of music were invalidated by the former's creation of such works as "The Raven, " which were experiments in sound but incorporated little meaning or real poetic value and by the latter's poem "The Symphony, " in which he fails in his seeming attempt to suggest verbally the sound of orchestral instruments.   It is the opinion of this writer that these admittedly flawed creative products do not negate the possible worth of their creators' theories.

Side by side with the suggestions of Poe and Lanier, let us examine the fascinating idea presented by Ned Rorem[16] that not only do the contours of vocal music depend on the language being set, but that instrumental music as well takes its shape from a nation's speech (and thereby, in a further extension of the hypothesis, resembles the people).   If this were true, would it not validate Lanier's notion about the "tunes" of speech and make it likely that these formulations

14

might subliminally be taken into a composer's palette of available sounds? Might it not also explain why the "tunes" and rhythms of American speech and poetry are different not only from German and French but also from British speech and poetry, and why the most convincing artistic products arise when the poetry and music of a song have the same national origins?

Although the scope of the subject is too great for the present volume, the author strongly supports for future inquiry the possibility that rhythmic patterns, tone color, melodic interval choice, and perhaps even harmonic structure in the American art song may indeed be linked to American speech and thereby have a common source that contributes to an American style.

Finally, as we approach consideration of the meaning of words as one of the most important aspects of their musical setting, we find that as great a poet as T. S. Eliot insists on the total integration in poetry of meaning with sound elements. In his treatise The Music of Poetry (originally a lecture delivered at the University of Glasgow), he maintains that "the music of poetry is not something which exists apart from the meaning" and furthermore that "a musical poem is a poem which has a musical pattern of sound and a musical pattern of the secondary meaning of the words which compose it, and that these two patterns are indissoluble and one. "[17]

However one feels about meaning in its relation to "music" in poetry, there is no doubt that the meaning does exist--that words have associations that have nothing or at least very little to do with their physical sound components. Opinion is not nearly as unanimous on the question of meaning in music. Calvin S. Brown holds that music differs from poetry in that there is no counterpart in music to the associative meanings of words.[18] Others disagree. Donald Ferguson and Deryck Cooke have written books called Music as Metaphor[19] and The Language of Music,[20] respectively. Edward MacDowell delivered a lecture called "Suggestion in Music"[21] (now published with others in book form) while teaching at Columbia University. All of these[22] attempt to show at some length and with numerous examples how specific musical elements, such as pitch, rhythm, volume, or harmony, have been traditionally used by composers in an activity often termed "word painting" to portray not only emotional states but also such specific concepts as direction, types of motion, light and darkness, water, and many others.

In the opinion of this writer, this metaphoric musical language not only has a very definite existence but also figures strongly in what we have come to be familiar with as the art song style of word setting, no matter what the language of the poetry. It is, in fact, a very important factor in our perception of the composer's choices as appropriate or inappropriate and thereby in our judgment of the song as a success or failure. The only area of art song in which this would perhaps not be true are some contemporary examples in which the words are used purely as sound elements without associative meaning, the question then arising as to whether these compositions still belong to the category of art song or should rather be considered chamber music with the voice as a participating instrument.

By threading our way through what we have now seen to be a considerable body, indeed, of principally American writings on the relationship of text and music, we have arrived at two summarizing, and analogous, concepts: the "music" of poetry and the "meaning" of music. Granting that the two art forms do have many elements in common, what do we find happening to the integrity of each in their coming together? The aesthetician Susanne K. Langer has formulated "the principle of assimilation, " in which she describes the process of writing a good song as a transformation of all verbal material (both sound and meaning) into musical elements. [23] Perhaps it is this view, which suggests the poetry disappearing into the music, that has led many poets of the past to reject even the greatest settings of their works, believing that they had been not only "assimilated" but destroyed.

Donald Ivey points the way to a resolution of the words/music dichotomy with a concept of equal function. Song, he suggests, "is a true hybrid in which both art forms relinquish some but not all of their individual characteristics. Even though the poem may lose its original poetic form when taken into a song, the words do not lose their function as language. " He also points out that although the form and content of the poetry and that of the music exist independently, they nevertheless function concurrently, and that "if the emotion aroused by the music is compatible with the emotion aroused by the poetry, the images have synthesized and the expressive experience is complete. "[24]

16

American poets of this century seem to welcome song composers rather than to resent them. e. e. cummings expressed admiration for Nordoff's settings of his poems[25] as did Wallace Stevens for Vincent Persichetti's Harmonium. Stevens, in fact, felt that Persichetti's cyclical treatment in this work illuminated some aspects of the poetry in a way that was only possible in music.[26] Paul Goodman also described himself as deeply moved by Ned Rorem's settings, and there are a number of American poets today who are interested in writing poetry for the express purpose of having it set to music.[27] Perhaps these writers have come to believe, as does this author, that the best songs are a true union between the individual characteristics of poetry and music, in which, as in all loving unions, neither is lost but each is fully realized in the other.

NOTES

1. Susanne K. Langer, Feeling and Form (New York: Scribner's, 1953), p. 154. The source of the original quotation also appears here.

2. Nordoff interview.

3. Persichetti interview.

4. Ned Rorem in an interview with the author at his home, New York City, April 16, 1975.

5. Calvin S. Brown, Music and Literature (Athens: University of Georgia Press, 1948), p. 46.

6. Donald Ivey, Song: Anatomy, Imagery, and Styles (New York: Free Press, 1970), p. 5.

7. Sidney Lanier, The Science of English Verse (New York: Scribner's, 1893, pp. 73 ff.

8. Brown, p. 20.

9. Letter from John Duke to the author, June 18, 1961.

10. Ivey, pp. 78 ff.

11.   Lawrence Gilman, Edward MacDowell, A Study (New York: Da Capo Press,   1969), p. 163.   This book, in the Da Capo Reprint Series, was originally published in 1908.

12.   Laurence Perrins, Literature--Structure, Sound, and Sense (New York: Harcourt, Brace and World, 1970), pp. 689 ff.

13.   Lanier, pp. 47 ff.

14.   Edgar Allan Poe, "The Poetic Principle, " in American Poetry and Poetics, ed. Daniel G. Hoffman (Garden City, New York: Doubleday, 1962), p. 305.

15.   Ivey, pp. 82 ff.

16.   Ned Rorem, Music from Inside Out (New York: Braziller, 1967), p. 59.

17.   T. S. Eliot, The Music of Poetry (Glasgow: Jackson, Son and Co. , 1942), pp. 18-19.

18.   Brown, p. 14.

19.   Donald Ferguson, Music as Metaphor (Minneapolis: University of Minnesota Press, 1960).

20.   Deryck Cooke, The Language of Music (London: Oxford University Press, 1959).

21.   Edward MacDowell, "Suggestion in Music, " in Critical and Historical Essays, ed. W. J. Baltzell (Boston: Stanhope Press, 1912).

22.   Ivey also has many examples of the use of melody, harmony, and rhythm to articulate the text (Chapters 5-7).

23.   Langer, p. 150.

24.   Ivey, pp. 95-96.

25.   Nordoff interview.

26.   Persichetti interview.

27.   Rorem interview.

18

II. TURN-OF-THE-CENTURY FIGURES

MacDowell, Loeffler, and Griffes were all born in the second half of the nineteenth century, when the aesthetic of German Romanticism and the mystique of German musical training still retained a firm grip on the musical thinking of Western Europe and America. All three of these composers received an important part of their preparation in Germany, and their songs for the most part reflect the lied tradition in poetic atmosphere and musical language.

Some intimations of a newly emerging synthesis can be sensed, however, as each composer infuses the existent tradition with his unique contributions. MacDowell draws on his Celtic ancestry and sense of dramatic simplicity. Loeffler demonstrates an uncanny rapport with the burning lyricism of Poe and the ability to translate it into musical terms. Griffes adds the colors of French Impressionism to his expanding palette and also experiments with an austerity of style that, in its response to the starkness of John Tabb's verses, seems like an early stirring of twentieth-century neoclassicism. The winds of change, then, are already rising as the old century ushers in the new.

Edward MacDowell (1861-1908)
William Dean Howells (1837-1920)

Although Edward MacDowell maintains his historical position

19

as the first American composer to achieve an international reputation, critical judgment of his music has fluctuated widely during the last seventy-five years from adulatory[1] to patronizing[2] and contemptuous,[3] with a balanced synthesis only recently beginning to emerge.[4] His songs have had a similar fate, for although Finck, during MacDowell's lifetime, named him as one of the two greatest living song writers (Grieg was the other),[5] the ensuing decades of the twentieth century brought little but neglect. Finally, the last fifteen years saw a reissuing of five opus numbers (including the Howells settings) in the Earlier American Music series[6] and the recording of a number of MacDowell songs.[7]

That his solo songs comprise ten opus numbers out of his published fifty-four attests to the importance of song writing to this composer. Yet these songs did not come to him in an easy, natural, Schubertian flow, but were instead the products of long and tortured analysis of the relationship between words and music. Despite--or perhaps as a result of --his being a sometime poet, MacDowell was convinced that "language and music have nothing in common," although he had "made many experiments for finding their affinity."[8] This conviction led him, interestingly, not to abandon the song medium, but to attempt to reduce its disabilities in two principal ways: first, by writing many texts himself, since he was able to find very little poetry that to him seemed suitable for setting, and second, by making the accompaniment "merely a background for the words," so that "the attention of the bearer should be fixed upon the central point of declamation."[9] The latter goal, that of concentrating on literary values, is well served by the basic song style that MacDowell evolved: a well-conceived vocal line of relative simplicity supported by the sustained chord type of accompaniment in which characteristic motifs are rarely if ever employed. It is less well served by the composer's strong tendency toward word repetition and distortion of syllabic accent. One wonders, on comparing MacDowell's songs with those of later American composers, whether it was the rigidity of much tradition-bound nineteenth-century poetry that led him to despair of any true correspondence between music and poetry or whether it was rather an innate lack of the ability, so essential to a song composer, to assimilate or blend their disparate elements into a new and meaningful whole.

In the settings of William Dean Howells's poetry that

occur among the eight songs of opus 47, we find some of MacDowell's most successful instances of musical correspondence to poetic ideas, despite his avowed aim being more likely the suppression of musical factors than their directed employment. His choice of Howells as a poet is interesting in itself, since this "dean" of nineteenth-century American letters made his creative reputation primarily as a writer of novels and essays. At the same time, he was also occupied successively as editor of the <u>Atlantic Monthly</u>, <u>Harper's</u>, and <u>Cosmopolitan</u>, and it was undoubtedly while living in Boston in association with the first of these positions that his contacts with MacDowell were formed. [10] Howells began his literary career as a poet, and while his early attempts in this medium tend to be weakened by formal clichés and Victorian sentimentality, the author's return to poetry in later life evidenced a considerable growth in originality and depth of feeling.

This growth is clearly demonstrated in the three poems that MacDowell set in opus 47. "Through the Meadow" and "Gone" (MacDowell changes the latter's title to "Folksong") both appear in an early collection published in 1873, when Howells was thirty-seven. Although MacDowell uses only fourteen lines of the original twenty-two in "Through the Meadow," the omission is not enough to mitigate the cloying nature of the poetry, which the composer's pleasant but undistinguished melodic line does not disguise. "Folksong" is a somewhat stronger poem and a better setting, for the change of title indicates that MacDowell had caught the elemental, folk flavor of the girl and her departing lover. The composer's penchant for uncluttered melody and chordal accompaniment reinforce this flavor, as do the ABA form, the minor key, and the rhythmic reference to Celtic folk song in the "Scotch-snap" at the beginning of measure five:

Example 2.1, measures 4-5.

A rare example of word painting for this composer occurs in the B section of "Folksong," in which the text describes the fading sound of the lover's horse and his disappearance from sight. MacDowell repeats "grow faint" and "has passed" two times each, over indicated diminuendos, in an obvious musical imitation of the diminishing sound and view of the rider. At the same time, the melodic line, which opens with a trumpet-call reference, is reharmonized on its repetition to create greater pathos through increased chromaticism, ending with a diminished chord on the word "sight."

Example 2.2, measures 10-17.

In the final stanza of this poem, Howells loses the strong simplicity of the other two in overblown language and an antiquated syllabic separation:

> She presses her tremulous fingers tight
> Against her closéd eyes,
> And on the lonesome threshold there,
> She cowers down and cries.

MacDowell cannot overcome this, but he lightens the onus by raising a minor third to a major at the beginning and end of this section (on "presses" and on the final word "cries"), which has the effect of lessening the personal involvement and opening out to a more universalized feeling, perhaps through our sublimated recognition of the Baroque "Picardy third" convention. [11]

"The Sea" is a later poem, and with it Howells has come into his own. The language is concise and forthright, there is not a trace of sentimentality, and the poetic form is an unusual one in which the last stanza effectively adds an extra poetic foot to the first line. MacDowell's setting matches the quality of the poetry. Folk elements are again utilized to some extent for this age-old subject of a lover lost at sea. The 6/8 meter and opening dotted rhythmic pattern ($\sqrt{.}$ $\sqrt{}$ $\sqrt{.}$ $\sqrt{}$) suggest a swinging sea-chanty; the Scotch-snap recurs in the grace notes of the melody;[12] the repetition of the simple ABA form is again the structural choice. But combined with these folk-like elements are the more sophisticated ones that give this song its unique character. The melodic line begins with the stepwise, narrow-range patterns typical of MacDowell but lunges into three full-octave leaps at the words "On the sullen water dies," while at the same time the diatonic harmony of the opening pulls to a tortuous chromatic bass line and chord structures (see Example 2. 3).

The accompaniment, unlike the other Howells settings, uses widely spaced chords with many octave doublings in the bass, all of which lend the larger dimension of an orchestral sonority. The key is surprisingly major (the usual choice for a sad folktale would be the minor mode), and in the coda that results from a text repetition of the last two lines plus the final word once again, MacDowell effectively underlines the tragedy of the lover's death with a melodic lowered sixth on "coral" and a poignant secondary dominant chord just before the last "asleep."

23

Example 2.3, measures 7-10.

Example 2.4, measures 29-35.

Charles Martin Loeffler (1861-1935)
Edgar Allan Poe (1809-1849)

___

Born in Alsace, Charles Martin Loeffler was an American by adoption. Loeffler, who was one of Joachim's[13] favorite pupils, studied the violin in Russia and France and played professionally in a private European chamber orchestra before he came to this country at the age of twenty. It is true that he was then to spend his remaining fifty-four years in America, until 1903 as first-desk player with the Boston Symphony, and thereafter as composer and recluse on his Massachusetts farm. Yet it is not the overwhelming proportion of American years to European years that merits Loeffler's position in this study. It is rather his remarkable affinity for the poetry of the pivotal and enigmatic Edgar Allan Poe and the resultant power of the two Poe settings that appeared in Loeffler's Four Poems Set to Music of 1906.[14]

As regards the details of their lives, these two artists were far apart, indeed. The composer had a stable home life and a long, successful career as an orchestral musician, and died, probably in his bed, at a ripe old age. The poet battled poverty and personal tragedy all of his life and died under mysterious circumstances in a Baltimore hospital at forty. Nevertheless, a study of their creative influences, goals, and methods reveals a surprising number of connections. France is perhaps the first and most obvious link. Loeffler, who studied with Debussy's teacher, Ernest Guirand, at the Paris Conservatory and maintained a lifelong friendship with Fauré, certainly derived a great deal stylistically from the Impressionistic palette. Moreover, as a devotee of French literature,[15] he set the poetry of Verlaine and Baudelaire and based a symphonic poem on a work of Maeterlinck. It is not surprising that he would be drawn to Edgar Allan Poe, whose writings influenced Debussy and Maeterlinck profoundly, and who, as the following quotation indicates, has been awarded by literary historians a seminal role in the Symbolist movement: "French Symbolism, with its desire to gain the suggestiveness of music, began at the moment when Baudelaire recognized in Poe's logical formulas for a poem his own half-developed thoughts combined to perfection."[16]

French civilization is a strong connection between the two men, but there are others. Although Poe's life span falls well within the flush of early Romanticism and Loeffler's certainly does not, both men show a deep involvement with the nineteenth-century predilections for "olden times" (Loeffler was a medievalist), exotic settings, fantasy, and the macabre. As counterparts to Poe's "Annabel Lee," "The Raven," "Masque of the Red Death," and "Fall of the House of Usher," Loeffler's creative catalog includes The Fantastic Concerto for cello and orchestra; La Villanelle du Diable (the devil's villanelle), an orchestral work; a symphony called Hora Mystica showing strong plainchant influence; and Pagan Poem for chamber group based on Virgil's Eighth Eclogue, in which a girl attempts sorcery to bring her lover back. [17] This tendency toward highly imaginative and often demonic fantasy coupled with the sensuous appeal of Loeffler's lush harmonies and Poe's onomatopoetic syllables brought similar critical salvos: Loeffler was called a "decadent" by Philip Hale (who later decided that his decadence was irrelevant), [18] and Poe was excoriated by his own literary executor, the Reverend Rufus Griswold, as a veritable monster who showed "scarcely any virtue in his life or writings." [19] With the passage of time, the qualities that were little understood by their contemporaries have emerged as the particular artistic strength of these men, that is, the ability to combine a free-flowing Romantic sweep of ideas with the tightest technical control over all aspects of the material.

In considering any settings of Edgar Allan Poe, one's first thought might be whether or not his poetry, which is so rich in verbal music, will lend itself to song, or whether the composer will indeed find nothing to add to the mellifluous sounds and well-developed imagery. Further reflection, however, leads one to the realization that the poems Loeffler has chosen--"A Dream Within a Dream" and "To Helen"--are among Poe's tersest lyrics, which, by virtue of short lines and thoughts suggested rather than fully stated, provide considerable scope for musical amplification. Loeffler, unlike MacDowell, does not repeat even one word of the poetry; the verses appear to the syllable as Poe wrote them. Also unlike MacDowell, Loeffler chooses to embed the text in a decorative and often polyphonic instrumental texture that, particularly in "A Dream Within a Dream," is reminiscent of the sweeping arpeggios and broad melodic lines in octaves that occur in the piano part of his Two Rhapsodies for oboe, viola and piano. [20]

"A Dream Within a Dream," written when Poe was only eighteen, is a tight, powerful poetic statement of an al-

ready full-blown existential despair over human destiny:
total extinction after a life that has much suffering but little
more reality or purpose than a dream. Loeffler opens his
setting with a pianistic figure repeated several times in ris-
ing sequence, which by virtue of its rhythmic repetition sug-
gests an almost hypnotic, dreamlike atmosphere, but whose
offbeat accents in the bass line lend a feeling of uneasiness.

Example 2. 5, measures 1-3. Copyright © 1906, G. Schir-
mer, Inc.; used by permission.

The overall rhythmic scheme of 12/8 (occasionally changing
to 9, 8, or 6 beats per measure) proves a very flexible ve-
hicle for the interesting and irregular poetic meter. Rhythm
is also used to convey the poet's growing anxiety as the
eighth notes break up into wildly rushing sixteenths.

Increasing harmonic instability reinforces the rhythmic
push. A relatively diatonic opening in D-flat major moves
to traditional cadences in the keys of the dominant and sub-
dominant, which become heavily decorated with nonchord
tones. The tension continues to mount with enharmonic
modulations and increased chromaticism, which culminates
in the piano interlude following "can I not save one from the
pitiless wave?" (see Example 2. 6). At the same time, the
vocal line has shown growing contrapuntal interaction with
the piano, and the pianistic melody has swelled from an
opening narrow-range chant to a broad, fortissimo series
of octaves. All of this tension finds musical release in the
postlude following the final refrain ("Is all that we see or
seem / But a dream within a dream?") with a return to
the rocking pattern of the opening, which seems to suggest
a retreat from anguished cerebration to a dreamlike state.

27

Example 2.6, measures 37-38. Copyright © 1906, G. Schirmer, Inc.; used by permission.

"To Helen," which dates from 1831, when Poe was twenty-two years old, is one of his finest lyrics. With surprising compression and great elegance of choice in poetic meter, rhyme scheme, and imagery, the Romantic artist's concept of Woman as a refuge from the storms of life and as an inspiration toward the noblest impulses of his own intellect and emotions[21] is set forth with great power. Loeffler utilizes his exquisite sense of harmonic appropriateness and considerable skill in motivic manipulation to create a seemingly "inevitable" setting.

One of the composer's effective devices is to lengthen the time value of the last syllable of each line. This affords the opportunity for the pianistic counterpoint to grow into lush melodic lines, which often derive from previous vocal or instrumental material. The Romantic excitement of the poem is underlined by what we have come to recognize, perhaps only subliminally at times, as typical nineteenth-century harmonic procedures: modulation to the mediant (F major going to A major before the first piano interlude), the sudden introduction of a lowered-sixth chord after a rallentando for textual emphasis (see Example 2.7), and the climactic treatment of the final poetic line. This treatment includes a fortissimo accompaniment in octave triplets and a chromatic rising vocal curve that diminuendos to an unexpected thirteenth chord (see Example 2.8). Loeffler now writes another postlude, which this time takes the form of a long winding-down after a burst of melody, in a manner reminiscent of Duparc's "Phidylé." Like the best of the Schumann postludes, this one has the effect of reinforcing the emotional content of

28

Example 2.7, measures 33-34. Copyright © 1906, G.
Schirmer, Inc.; used by permission.

Example 2.8, measures 39-40. Copyright © 1906, G.
Schirmer, Inc.; used by permission.

the song at least partially through the return of motivic material.

Finally, it should be said that the principal motivic material, just referred to for the second time, consists of a descending chromatic line,

thy beau - ty is to me

Example 2.9, measures 4-5. Copyright © 1906, G. Schirmer, Inc.; used by permission.

and a rising series that combines whole- and half-steps:

To his own na - tive shore. _____

Example 2.10, measures 12-13. Copyright © 1906, G. Schirmer, Inc.; used by permission.

Both of these reappear at many pitch levels, in varying rhythmic contexts, and with changing harmonic backgrounds, and it is impossible to miss the yearning quality imparted by the sliding chromatics, particularly when incorporated in the rising line.

Charles Griffes (1884-1920)
John Tabb (1845-1909), Sidney Lanier (1842-1881)

Although his tragically short life cut off the promise of still further development, Charles Griffes nevertheless created during his thirty-six years a body of compositions that marks him as one of the major American composers of the early twentieth century. No lesser authority than Gilbert Chase, the elder statesman of American musical historians, puts the case succinctly in these terms: "[Griffes's] major works are American classics; his songs are among the best we have."22

30

It must also be said, to the credit of the musical public, that the well-deserved reputation of Griffes's songs seems never to have been in dispute. William Treat Upton writing in Art Song in America, which was published only ten years after the composer's death, presented a treatment of his style that is remarkable for its thoroughness and insight into Griffes's great strengths as a song composer. [23] Performances of the songs, however, which proliferated during the composer's lifetime, [24] diminished thereafter except for the anthologized "By a Lonely Forest Pathway"[25] and "The Lament of Ian the Proud."[26] In 1966, recordings began to appear, [27] and two scholarly studies that involve Griffes songs have now been written: a descriptive catalog of all the Griffes works[28] and a master's thesis on the songs alone. [29]

Charles Griffes, according to all we know of his life and interests, was an artist who was open to not only the new musical trends of his time as represented by Debussy, Scriabin, Stravinsky, Schoenberg, and Varèse, but also to influences from Oriental and European cultures. In addition, he showed considerable skill in sketching and photography. It is particularly interesting in the context of this wide-ranging sensibility to note the American poets that Griffes chose for setting and to speculate on their attraction for him. His biographer, Maisel, mentions that Griffes "was much interested in the new American poetry movement,"[30] but the evidence consists of only a single song: Sara Teasdale's "Pierrot" (unpublished), written in 1912, [31] which is a light-textured, serenade-type setting somewhat reminiscent of Debussy's "Mandoline" but less harmonically subtle--in all, a work of some charm but little depth, like the poem. This, then, was Griffes's only venture into the American poetry of his contemporaries, and apparently he found it an unfruitful field for his own inspiration. His other American settings, all of which date from 1911 and 1912, consist of one poem by Sidney Lanier and five by John Tabb, both of whom were born approximately forty years before the composer.

The songs that we shall examine of this group are three that were refused publication by G. Schirmer in 1912 (along with "Pierrot") but were finally published by the same company in 1941: "Evening Song, " the Lanier poem, and "The Half-Ring Moon" and "The First Snowfall, " two poems by John Tabb. Two other Tabb settings, called "Phantom"

31

and "The Water-Lily, " which remain in manuscript, [32] show instances of Griffes's skill as a sensitive harmonic colorist but suffer from the weakness of the poems. These are over-blown, conventional apostrophes to falling snow and a flower, respectively, whose Victorian language is at war with the Impressionistic chord structures of the settings. Indeed, in most of the songs circa 1912, Griffes was turning away from the Brahms-Strauss influence of his 1901 Five German Poems and absorbing into his style many of the new French elements then making their way across the Atlantic.

John Tabb is a little-known American poet, native to Virginia, who was born an Episcopalian but who after years of soul-searching converted to Catholicism. Ordained as a priest, he nevertheless held no parish, and taught English literature all his life. While serving as a blockade runner in the Civil War, he was captured and sent to Point Look-out, where he met a fellow prisoner, Sidney Lanier. The two became lifelong friends, and Tabb helped to direct Lanier toward his eventual adoption of a serious career as a poet. Another coincidence meaningful to this study is the strong absorption of both men in music, for Tabb would have become a professional musician had his eyes not been weak from an early age, and Lanier played almost all in-struments as a child and served as first flautist in the Pea-body Orchestra of Baltimore in the early 1870s. Similar-ities end, however, in the area of poetic style and artistic goals, and the differences we shall find clearly delineated in the three posthumous songs of 1941.

Standing quite apart from the diffuse style of most of his contemporaries, and particularly those of the South, John Tabb worked throughout his life in the direction of poetic clarity and concision. "His ability to say much in little, to suggest profound thought by a single word, has been recog-nized by all critics, " says Francis Litz, Tabb's editor. [33] This seeming simplicity, together with a polished technique and a tendency toward religious overtones in concept and imagery, is strongly reminiscent of Emily Dickinson, whose works might well have been known by Tabb in his maturity, since he was forty-five at the time of the first publication of her poetry (1890).

The settings of "The Half-Ring Moon" and "The First Snowfall" are as concise as the poetry: for each eight-line poem Griffes has composed two pages of music, running twenty measures in each case. "The Half-Ring Moon" is a fairly early poem (1884), which in its few short lines tells a story of a lover who comes no more over the sea, but whose pledge of love, the half of a golden ring, can be seen hanging in the sky. On hearing this setting, one is struck by the fact that the accompaniment figure seems to hark back to Griffes's German songs in its Brahmsian wide-spaced chords and two-against-three rhythmic patterns. It is perhaps a bit heavy for the folkish character of the poem, but the song is redeemed by its considerable harmonic interest. A constant wavering between major and minor colorings and a prolonged emphasis on the VI chord before the final introduction of the E minor tonic lend an archaic flavor that matches the poetic atmosphere of such lines as "My love he is gone to a far countrie." Also the enormous skill as a writer of counter-melodies in the piano part, which Griffes shares equally with Loeffler, is used for dramatic effect in underlining the pathos of the climactic line "He comes no more from the far countrie":

Example 2.11, measures 11-14. Copyright © 1941, G. Schirmer, Inc.; used by permission.

"The First Snowfall" shows John Tabb at his best in a laconic, Dickinson-like observation that the same snowfall is at once life-giving to the fir tree and a messenger of death to the last falling leaf. Griffes's setting, which Hans Nathan finds to have several "intriguing aspects,"[34] is as austere as the poem and creates most of its effect through the harmonic means of Impressionism. These include non-resolving chord tones added for coloristic effect, pedal points to contribute a tonal orientation, and Griffes's own instruction that the piano part is to be "veiled through a constant use of both pedals" (una corda and damper). The last few measures of the piece are illustrative of these elements, as well as of the relatively simple and diatonic melodic line, which mirrors the leanness of the text.

Example 2.12, measures 17-20. Copyright © 1941, G. Schirmer, Inc.; used by permission.

For Sidney Lanier's "Evening Song," Griffes returns to the full, chordal accompaniment of his "German period" and adopts many of the lush, nineteenth-century harmonic procedures that Loeffler utilized in setting Lanier's poetic counterpart, Edgar Allan Poe. The altered chords, the chromatic sideslips to foreign keys, modulations to the third, and frustrated harmonic goals of motion all intensify the rush of emotion in this "spontaneous yet controlled" lyric, in which Lanier finally found the perfect expression he had been seeking of his feeling for his wife.[35] In truth, this powerful setting, which Griffes's unerring color sense placed in the key of C-sharp minor so that its many sharps might impart a quality of ecstatic brightness, is a perfect representation of all the characteristics of the composer's style that lend it to greatness. These include the inherent beauty and textual appropriateness of the melodic and harmonic choices, and his seemingly effortless ability to adapt poetic meter to musical structure (there are no word repetitions and no important deletions in any of these songs). Still another strength is his fine instinct for form, which here involves a much-modified ABA structure for the three stanzas of verse and also includes an effective repetition of the introductory material transposed before verse three.

Lanier has been denigrated by critics through the years for his tendency to sentimentality and lack of intellectual control. There is, however, little question that he, like Poe, made his very considerable poetic contributions through his great sensitivity to patterns of sound, and his ability to communicate "the excitement of music to verse."[36] In "Evening Song," Griffes reconverts this excitement into actual musical terms. One example is the tentative opening figure, in which the tonic chord in its major and minor form alternates with tension-producing dissonant neighboring chords:

Example 2.13, measures 1-3. Copyright © 1941, G. Schirmer, Inc.; used by permission.

Another is the chromatic sidestep to a B-flat chord on the word "sun," which in its creation of a sense of wonder through a sudden move to a foreign harmony is very evocative of Schumann's Dichterliebe (see Example 2.14). A third is the setting of "Cleopatra night drinks all, Tis done," in which the moment of suspense before the sun drops into the sea is given exquisite musical expression. Griffes de-

35

And watch yon meet - ing of sun ____ and sea, ____ How

Example 2.14, measures 7-8. Copyright © 1941, G. Schirmer, Inc.; used by permission.

lays the expected resolution of the V chord by the interruption of an altered VI with an appoggiatura, before it returns to the tonic (Verse two is cadencing at this point in E major):

Cle - o - pa - tra night ____ drinks

all.   'Tis done, ____

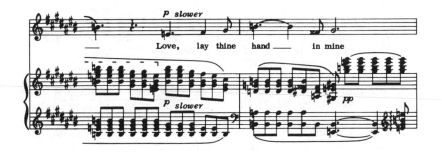

Example 2.15, measures 17-21. Copyright © 1941, G.
Schirmer, Inc.; used by permission.

Finally, the postlude begins its passionate outburst
with a pianistic appoggiatura similar to the one just quoted,
which musically unites that former moment of deep emotion
with the final prayerful exhortation:

> "O night! divorce our sun and sky apart,
> Never our lips, our hands."

Example 2.16, measures 35-36. Copyright © 1941, G.
Schirmer, Inc.; used by permission.

NOTES

1. Lawrence Gilman, Edward MacDowell, A Study (New York: DaCapo Press, 1969), Chapter III, "His Art and Its Methods." This book in the DaCapo Reprint Series was originally published in 1908.

2. Daniel Gregory Mason in Contemporary Composers (New York: Macmillan, 1918), p. 276: "His range of expression ... is not wide, and within it he frequently cloys by an over-sweet sentimentalism. But MacDowell is sincere and he is always himself.... His style is very narrow but it is his own."

3. Paul Rosenfeld in chapter on MacDowell found in An Hour with American Music (Philadelphia: Lippincott, 1929): "Where his great romantic brethren, Brahms, Wagner, and Debussy, are direct and sensitive, clearly and tellingly expressive, MacDowell minces and simpers, maidenly and ruffled. He is nothing if not a daughter of the American Revolution."

4. John Tasker Howard in Our American Music (New York: Crowell, 1965), p. 325: "MacDowell is probably the first of our creative musicians for whom we need make no allowances for lack of early training. None of his limitations was caused by his being an American.... And after we have put him under the magnifying glass, stripped him of ... idealization ... he will emerge with several of his banners still flying."

5. Henry T. Finck, Songs and Song Writers (New York: Scribner's, 1900), p. 240.

6. H. Wiley Hitchcock (ed.), Earlier American Music, vol. 7 (New York: DaCapo Press, 1972).

7. a) John K. Hanks and Ruth C. Friedberg, Art Song in America, vol. I (Durham, North Carolina: Duke University Press, 1966). Contains "Thy Beaming Eyes, " "Long Ago, Sweetheart Mine, " and "The Sea. " b) Songs of American Composers (Desto Records). "The Sea" sung by John Mc-Collum, tenor. c) Recorded Anthology of American Music (New World Records, 1976). Reissues of 1912 performances by Alma Gluck of "Long Ago, Sweetheart Mine" and "A Maid Sings Light. "

8. An interview with MacDowell quoted by Gilman, p. 164.

9. Ibid., p. 163.

10. Howells was in Boston from 1865 to 1891, and Mac-Dowell from 1888 to 1896. These terms of residence coincide from 1888 to 1891 and the Howells settings were published in 1893, hence the author's hypothesis.

11. The common Baroque practice of ending a work in the minor mode with a major chord or phrase.

12. The recurrence of this rhythmic motif recalls Mac-Dowell's Celtic ancestry.

13. Joseph Joachim (1831-1907) was a German violinist and teacher of great renown.

14. These songs are currently out of print. "A Dream Within a Dream" is recorded in Hanks and Friedberg, vol. L

15. Edwin Burlingame Hill, "Charles Martin Loeffler," Modern Music, vol. 13, (November-December 1935), pp. 26-31.

16. Robert E. Spiller, Willard Thorpe, Thomas J. Johnson, Henry Seidel Canby, and Richard M. Ludwig (eds.), Literary History of the United States (New York: Macmillan, 1963), p. 340.

17. For a fuller description of Loeffler's works, see Howard, pp. 349-351.

18. Philip Hale's critical comments are discussed in Carl Engel, "Charles Martin Loeffler," Musical Quarterly, vol. 2, no. 3 (July 1925), p. 320.

19. Spiller, et al., p. 321.

20. Charles Martin Loeffler, Two Rhapsodies for oboe, viola, and piano (New York: Schirmer, 1932). Now out of print.

21. For a different interpretation of this poem, which suggests the egocentricity of its message, see Hyatt H. Wag-

goner, American Poets from the Puritans to the Present (New York: Dell, 1968), p. 141.

22. Gilbert Chase, America's Music (New York: McGraw-Hill, 1966), p. 522.

23. William Treat Upton, Art-Song in America (New York: Ditson, 1930; reprinted 1969, Johnson Reprint Corp.), pp. 265-266.

24. Considerable information on early performances of Griffes's songs can be found in the following references: a) Edward M. Maisel, Charles T. Griffes (New York: Knopf, 1943). b) Marion Bauer, "Charles Griffes as I Remember Him," Musical Quarterly, vol. 29 (July 1943), pp. 355-380. c) Donna Kay Anderson, The Works of Charles T. Griffes: A Descriptive Catalogue (Ann Arbor, Michigan: 1966 dissertation). An expanded version of this work has been published by the College Music Society in its Bibliographies in American Music. It is titled The Works of Charles T. Griffes: An Annotated Bibliography-Discography (1977, Donna K. Anderson).

25. This song appears in 50 Art Songs from the Modern Repertoire (New York: Schirmer, 1939).

26. This is in the collection called Songs by Twenty-two Americans, compiled by Bernard Taylor (New York and London: Schirmer, 1960).

27. a) Hanks and Friedberg. Contains "By a Lonely Forest Pathway, " "The Lament of Ian the Proud, " "Symphony in Yellow, " and "An Old Song Resung. " b) Songs of American Composers, "Waikiki, " sung by Eleanor Steber. c) Recorded Anthology of American Music. A complete disc (two sides) of selected songs and instrumental music by Griffes.

28. Anderson.

29. Carolyn Lambeth Livingston, The Songs of Charles T. Griffes (Chapel Hill: University of North Carolina master's thesis, 1947).

30. Maisel, p. 111.

31. Ms. in the Library of Congress.

40

32.   The manuscript of "Phantoms" is in the New York Public Library, and that of "The Water Lily" is in the Library of Congress.   The manuscript of still another Tabb setting, "Cleopatra and the Asp, " has been lost.

33.   Francis A. Litz (ed.), The Poetry of Father Tabb (New York: Dodd, Mead, 1928), p. vii.

34.   Hans Nathan, "The Modern Period--United States of America, " A History of Song, ed. Denis Stevens (New York: Norton, 1960), p. 428.

35.   Charles R. Anderson (ed.), Sidney Lanier, Poems and Poem Outlines (Baltimore: Johns Hopkins Press, 1945), p. lii.

36.   Spiller, et al. , p. 907.

III. CHARLES IVES (1874-1954)

Charles Ives stands alone. He belongs to no historical
"group," and indeed he resisted all influences except the
"still, small voice" within that drove him to a secret life of
innovative creativity that has become legend. The songs of
Charles Ives represent his stylistic development in micro-
cosm. They begin with traditional German and French set-
tings during the 1890s and grow increasingly "American" in
their orientation as well as increasingly experimental in all
elements of musical style.

Ives's songs, like the rest of his compositions, were
conceived in isolation and born into a hostile world. Never-
theless, these songs have become, in the half-century since
their original printing, a valued part of America's national
heritage. They were heralded in 1934 by Aaron Copland in
an article that was to prove an important opening wedge in
the recognition of Ives's work.[1] They have been explored
since in varying degrees by all the major Ives scholars and
chroniclers.[2] As yet unexplored, however, are the relation-
ships between Ives and those leading American poets of the
nineteenth and early twentieth centuries whose texts he had
begun to set soon after graduation from Yale, under the
growing conviction of having, in Emerson's words, "listened
too long to the courtly muses of Europe."[3]

Ralph Waldo Emerson was already well established as
one of Ives's heroes when as an undergraduate Ives listened
to Horatio Parker[4] expound on the philosophy of the "sage of
Concord." Ives even went so far as to submit a paper on
Emerson to a campus literary publication; in ironic prophecy

of disappointments to come, it was rejected. Emerson, in his writings on "Self Reliance" and "The American Scholar," sought to arouse courage and authenticity of thinking in his countrymen. Those qualities were early established in the young Ives by a father who encouraged musical experimentation and originality. In another pivotal essay, "The Poet," Emerson called for a new voice to express the soul of America, and Walt Whitman seemed to him to be the fulfillment of that prophecy. In Charles Ives's work, we find not only a continuation of the search to express America, but something that would have pleased Emerson equally: a translation into musical terms of Transcendentalism, his religio-philosophic system based on the oneness of nature, humanity, and God. [5]

The all-inclusiveness of this philosophy, which was deeply ingrained in Ives, accounts for both the coexistence (either successively or simultaneously) of very disparate elements in individual songs, and for the enormous range of style, mood, and text in the songs as a whole. Both of these types of diversity will be encountered in the following list of twelve songs to be discussed in this chapter. This list is given in chronological order of composition and indicates those instances (numbers 3 through 7) in which the original scoring was other than for voice and piano:

	Song	Poet	Original	Rescoring
1.	"The Children's Hour"	Longfellow	1901 voice & piano	--
2.	"The Light That Is Felt"	Whittier	1904 voice & piano	--
3.	"Serenity"	Whittier	1909 chorus & orchestra	1921 voice & piano
4.	"The Last Reader"	O. W. Holmes	1911 voice & chamber group	1921 voice & piano
5.	"The Indians"	Chas. Sprague	1912 voice & chamber group	1921 voice & piano

	Song	Poet	Original	Rescoring
6.	"Duty"	Emerson	1911/12/ 13(?) chorus & orchestra	1921 voice & piano
7.	"Walt Whit- man"	Whitman	1913 chorus & orchestra	1921 voice & piano
8.	"General Wm. Booth Enters into Heaven"	V. Lindsay	1914 voice & piano	--
9.	"Thoreau"	Thoreau	1915 voice & piano	--
10.	"The Swim- mers"	L. Unter- meyer	1915-21 voice & piano	--
11.	"Afterglow"	J. F. Coop- er, Jr.	1919 voice & piano	--
12.	"Maple Leaves"	T. B. Al- drich	1920 voice & piano	--

Although these twelve songs represent a span of twenty years, two important characteristics prevail throughout the list. The first is what might be termed a nonobservance of poetic integrity, which includes using fragments of larger poems, word repetition and omission, changes in word order or in the words themselves, and occasional retitling of the original poem. These practices by no means originated with Ives, and it is not surprising that a man who also set texts written by himself, his wife, newspaper journalists, and indeed anything that seemed appropriate to the overall goal of his broadened concept of musical expression, would approach the poetry of the masters in a similar context of "means toward an end." Set over against this, however, is the other characteristic of these songs, which is a careful and effective attention to the details of word setting that is in the finest tradition of art song composition and belies any suspicion of randomness that might arise from the poetic fragmentation.

"The Children's Hour" was written in 1901, when Ives was
three years out of Yale, living in New York as a bachelor
insurance clerk and spending his "spare" time as church or-
ganist, choirmaster, and composer. This song, by virtue
of its relatively few performance difficulties and the aptness
and elegance of its construction, has become one of the most
popular of the "114. "[6] However, like many another great
poetic setting, Ives's "Children's Hour" is quite different
from Longfellow's.

Henry Wadsworth Longfellow, along with Bryant,
Lowell, Holmes, and Whittier, falls into a group of nineteenth-
century writers who were our first actual American "poets, "
i. e. , men who were accepted as such both at home and
abroad. They are quite generally conceded to have been
minor figures, and their styles leaned heavily on models,
but each was to write a few poems that would become land-
marks for nineteenth-century America. Longfellow was born
in Portland, Maine, the son of an attorney and member of
Congress, and was educated at Bowdoin College. He had a
seemingly peaceful and rewarding life as a man of letters and
held professorships of modern languages successively at Bow-
doin and at Harvard University before retiring in 1854 to de-
vote himself exclusively to writing. But personal tragedy
did not spare the gentle scholar despite his reputation and
affluence. In 1831, his first wife died in childbirth. Thirty
years later, his second wife burned to death in their home
when her dress accidentally caught fire, and he was left with
five growing children, three of whom appear in this poem. [7]

The inconsistencies that marked his life are not ab-
sent from the poetry. Although in much of his work he
seems, in Walt Whitman's words, to be the poet of "sym-
pathetic gentleness" and "of the mellow twilight of the past, "
lurking just below the surface is the melancholy sense of
"time as inherently and inevitably man's enemy, bringing
only loss and nothingness. "[8] Even the "mellow twilight"
glow of "The Children's Hour, " with its golden merry little
girls, is eventually dispelled as the poet gives way to a
rather coy self-pity ("such an old mustache as I am") and
a despairing resolve to cling to the memory of this moment:

"In the round-tower of my heart...
Till the walls shall crumble to ruin
And moulder in dust away. "

Not surprisingly, Ives, in the full flush of his early
transcendental optimism, chose to set the delightful, living
moment and to omit all mention of its threatened dissolution.
Out of an original ten stanzas, he sets only three, and closes
with a shortened version of stanza one. This verbal repeti-
tion coincides with an ABA musical structure (the return to
A is also shortened), which Ives was to use rarely, particu-
larly in his later songs. There are other early style charac-
teristics evident here also, such as the diatonic harmony,
lyricism and chordal leaps of the melodic line, and conven-
tional metric schemes with much repetition of rhythmic pat-
terns. There is, in fact, a rhythmic ostinato used through-
out the first A section, whose softly hypnotic insistence pro-
vides an initial sense of the hush and quiet of twilight in the
days before electricity.

Example 3. 1, measures 1-2. Copyright 1933, Merion Mu-
sic, Inc.; used by permission.

This ostinato also serves a melodic function and at the same
time a harmonic one, as with the change of a very few notes,
chordal meanings are subtly shifted (see Example 3. 2).

Notice in Example 3. 2 how Ives provides, as a mir-
ror of the text, a 2 1/2-beat "pause" on the word "hour"
before continuing. As he enters the B section, the ostinato
disappears and a new triplet figure increases the urgency of

47

Example 3.2, measures 8-10.   Copyright 1933, Merion Music, Inc.; used by permission.

the piu moto indication as the text becomes alive with "the patter of little feet" and the sound of voices and of doors being opened.

Example 3.3, measures 11-12.   Copyright 1933, Merion Music, Inc.; used by permission.

Stanza 3, still musically in the B section, moves to a 6/8 rhythm, which provides an opportunity for interesting cross-accents between voice and piano (see Example 3.4).   The section climaxes with an unexpected key shift from D major to A-flat major that lends a fresh sound to the use of the rapid sixteenth-note triplet on the word "laughing."

The return of the section-A ostinato has the satisfying

Example 3.4, measures 15-19.   Copyright 1933, Merion Music, Inc.; used by permission.

effect of rounding off the picture that has been created and fixing it in place.   Ives's understated polytonal implication of overlapping G and A triads in the final measure creates an unresolved musical atmosphere that suggests not the nostalgia of memory but the permeation of the present moment by eternity.

Example 3.5, measures 25-27.   Copyright 1933, Merion Music, Inc.; used by permission.

John Greenleaf Whittier (1807-1892)

John Greenleaf Whittier, who had been a friend of Ives's father-in-law, also shared a New England heritage with the composer, as did almost all the leading American poets Ives was to set. He was born in Haverhill, Massachusetts, but into much less auspicious circumstances than was Longfellow, and as a consequence led a far different kind of life. Whittier, the son of a Quaker farmer, was largely self-educated. When his literary talents began to be evident, he plunged into a successful career as a newspaper editor and politician. He was an active abolitionist and a founder of the Republican party. In 1865, he served as a presidential elector. After the Civil War, however, his life became more that of the cloistered poet. At the age of seventy, he finally received recognition from the academic world as a man of letters in the form of honorary degrees from Haverford College and Harvard University.

Whittier's most successful poems are generally conceded to be those that reflect the life of the mid-nineteenth-century New England farmer. He is particularly effective when dealing with nature, childhood, and his deeply felt, relatively orthodox religious perceptions. All three of these categories, but principally the last, are represented in varying combinations in the two texts of his that Ives chose for setting. It is worthy of note that Whittier is the only leading American poet that Ives set more than once.

Religion was as strong an element in Ives's life as it was in Whittier's, not only as a focus of such activities as revival meetings, church organist positions, and the like, but also as a shaping force in all his thinking about human nature and destiny. Interestingly, in setting these two texts, both of which deal in direct, simple terms with the place of God in human life, Ives employs two completely different styles. These are like an example in microcosm of the change that was to take place in his writing around 1907.

"The Light That Is Felt" dates from 1904, [9] relatively the same period in Ives's life and composition as "The Children's Hour." It, too, is diatonic and in general falls into the category of Ives's "household songs," which H. Wiley Hitchcock describes as "pleasant to perform and to hear, and not too demanding technically."[10] But this song is deceptive

and in the same manner as the much later "Two Little Flow-
ers" (1921), in that it also contains details of style that prove
quite surprising in this context.   The first surprise occurs
in measure 4 in the form of a quite shocking chromatic al-
teration of the tonic B to B-sharp.   This creates an unex-
pected dissonance in both verses of the strophic setting with
no seeming textual origin (see Example 3.6, first measure).

        The next striking feature of the setting is its rhythmic
organization.   Ives has used the first two out of the three
stanzas in the original poem.   He has translated the some-
what unusual five-line verse form into a standard 2/4 meter,
but with an asymmetrical and arresting overall phrase struc-
ture, which has the following measure grouping:

                Verse I: 5,   5,   2

                Verse II: 5,   5,   3

The asymmetry is further emphasized by the fact that the
inner vocal phrases do not coincide with those of the arpeg-
giated accompaniment, the latter beginning frequently on
weak beats with a syncopated effect that is a direct parallel
to the piano part of "Two Little Flowers."

Example 3.6, measures 4-7.   Copyright 1950, Mercury Mu-
sic, Inc.; used by permission.

        Finally, Ives's small but cogent alterations in the
text of this poem must be noted.   In each verse, Ives re-
peats a short but emotionally climactic phrase (verse I: "O,

51

mother, take my hand"; verse II: "The night is day") and be-
gins the repetition with a striking octave leap upward. In
the second verse, Ives adds the word "then" rather than land
on the upper octave with an unsuitable "the."

Example 3. 7, measures 19-25. Copyright 1950, Mercury
Music, Inc.; used by permission.

Further, just before the repetition in verse II, Ives changes
the text from

> "and only when our hands we lay
> Dear Lord, in thine, the night is day,"

to the way it appears in example 3. 7, substituting "Oh, God"
for the weaker "Dear Lord," and shifting the word order for
even stronger musical effect.

The years 1907 and 1908 were pivotal ones for Charles
Ives. In 1907, he started his own insurance agency with

Julian Myrick, and in 1908, after an impatient courtship, married Harmony Twichell. The liberating effects of being in business for himself and having a mate who was constantly encouraging of his creative originality combined to make the next decade his most experimental and prolific. Performances of his works by the outside world, however, were very rare in this period, and in despair of finding singers who were able or willing to sing difficult intervals, Ives turned to setting texts for unison chorus and orchestra, or for voice and chamber group with the voice part sometimes being taken by an instrument (despite the notated text).

Songs 3 through 7 on the list originated in this fashion between 1909 and 1913 and will be discussed in order of their original composition, although they were not arranged for voice and piano until Ives gathered his 114 Songs for publication in 1921. "Serenity" began, in Ives's subtitle, as a "unison chant"--a Whitman-like concept, no doubt, of a people's chorus, for Ives was to believe in the fundamental goodness of the majority until the debacle of World War I and his physical collapse in 1918. In its solo form, it becomes a very intimate, meditative distillation of the soul yearning for inward peace: a transmutation of the Gregorian spirit into a twentieth-century frame of reference.

"Serenity" is Ives's title, not Whittier's, and no doubt derives from a hymn tune of the same name (based on another Whittier text), which Ives quotes at the end of both musical stanzas. 11 The text of Ives's song is two verses only out of seventeen that the poet had called "The Brewing of Soma. " The poem describes the use through the ages of "brews, " drugs, and many other forms of artificial stimulation to achieve mystic union with God. It closes with an affirmation of inner tranquility as the only truly receptive state for spiritual grace, and it is from this conclusion that Ives extracted the idea of "Serenity" that was to form his title and the all-pervading mood of the song. The chant-like atmosphere that Ives deemed appropriate to this mood is achieved by a combination of carefully controlled musical details. One is the stepwise melodic line with many repeated notes and subtle combinations of duple, triple, and syncopated rhythms (see Example 3. 8). Another is the shifting of melodic centers from G to F and back to G again, a process very reminiscent of liturgical chant despite the fact that the context is tonal rather than modal. The spare accompaniment figure of two repeating bell-like chords in the

Example 3. 8, measures 7-12. Copyright © 1957, Associated Music Publishers, Inc.; used by permission.

upper register reinforces the repetitive, hypnotic nature of the chant, and this pattern is interrupted only twice by the hymn quotation ending in a plagal cadence that occurs before each caesura (see Example 3. 8, last measure). One final detail in the exquisite craftsmanship of this song is the introduction of an extra accompaniment chord in measure 19, which shifts the direction of the harmonic movement and causes a lifting effect that is exactly appropriate to the poetic phrase.

Example 3. 9, measures 13-20. Copyright © 1957, Associated Music Publishers, Inc.; used by permission.

54

Oliver Wendell Holmes (1809-1894)

The setting of Oliver Wendell Holmes's "The Last Reader" originated as one of the "sets" (Ives's term for his songs with chamber orchestra); this 1911 version called for two flutes, cornet, violas, and organ. The poem is an interesting choice from several points of view, and the setting illustrates many aspects of Ives's style in this increasingly experimental period.

Oliver Wendell Holmes was Cambridge born and reared and Harvard educated. His life presents an interesting parallel to the composer's, in that he earned his living as a doctor and professor at Harvard Medical School while leading a second life as a writer of poetry and prose. Holmes's work, however, unlike Ives's, found no obstacle to publication in his lifetime, and he was widely esteemed for his poetry, essays, and lectures. There were many scientific papers as well, and it is perhaps not surprising that with the passage of time, Holmes turned increasingly to lighter subjects for his verse. His writing career, however, was of great importance to him, as is clear in the following statement from his essay collection The Poet at the Breakfast Table: "I should like to be remembered as having said something worth lasting, well enough to last."

In "The Last Reader," Holmes voices the disquieting possibility that oblivion might indeed fall on his "neglected songs" but is soothed by the thought that they will still have meaning to him as memories of his youth and "thoughts that once were mine." The title of the poem emerges from the last two lines:

"And give the worm my little store
When the last reader reads no more."

Despite the growing disillusion caused by the world's neglect, Ives once again, in 1911, chose only the most positive parts of this poem for setting (verses I and III out of a total of eight). He used the stanzas that describe how the poet's own verses bring him joy and even assuage the pain of old age, and discarded the somewhat morbid musings on death and oblivion. The last two lines (quoted above) do not appear in the song, which makes the title difficult to comprehend and causes some question as to why Ives did not change it, as he did so many others.

55

In the setting for voice and piano (number 3 in the 114 Songs), Ives indicates two quotations in the vocal line: one by Spohr, which opens the piece, and one in the third score, by Haydn. Ives's use of quotations had, of course, become an integral part of his mature writing, and in typical fashion, he quotes the melodies first in simple diatonic form and then proceeds to introduce chromatic alterations and dissonant chordal backgrounds.

Example 3.10a, measures 7-9. Copyright 1933, Merion Music, Inc.; used by permission.

Example 3.10b, measures 17-19. Copyright 1933, Merion Music, Inc.; used by permission.

The psychological genesis of the use of quotations here seems to be the poem's references to times past and "scarce re-

membered lays, " and Ives's interest in the past is well
known. It is also easy to see how he could have identified
at this period of his public neglect with Holmes's opening
lines:

> "I sometimes sit beneath a tree
> And read my own sweet songs;
> Though naught they may to others be...."

Whatever the sources of the poem's appeal, one finds
Ives involved in fascinating complexities in its setting. The
rhythmic structure at times mirrors the poetic feet with a
6/4 meter that imitates the iambic pattern, but as often de-
parts into a 3/4 or 4/4 meter that completely transforms
the original poetic accents and line arrangement.

Example 3.11, measures 1-3.   Copyright 1933, Merion Mu-
sic, Inc.; used by permission.

In the beginning of verse III ("As on a father's careworn
cheek") rhythmic groupings in the piano's left hand are or-
ganized to present a misty, uneven background flow behind
the more steadily moving voice line: an effective device but
one that is considerably challenging to the performers (see
Example 3.12).

Harmonic aspects of this song are equally interesting,
revealing an essentially diatonic vocal melody that embodies
a few surprising chromatic alterations in pursuit of subse-
quent key shifts, such as the change from a G center to B-
flat in measures 11 to 14 (Example 3.12).   Also notice in

measure 11, Example 3.12, that the B-flat triad is already
being expressed in the bass clef while the uppermost voice
suggests a G harmony and the middle voices, a gratuitous
C minor chord.

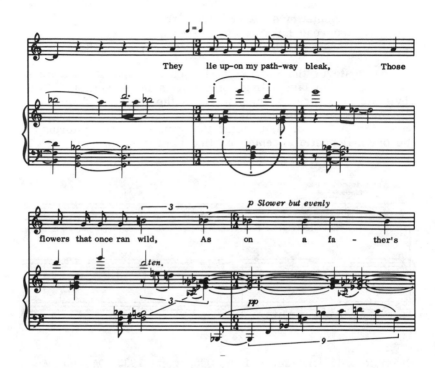

Example 3.12, measures 10-14. Copyright 1933, Merion
Music, Inc.; used by permission.

Ives's harmonic vocabulary in the accompaniment includes
milder augmented chords and more dissonant minor ninths
but all are muted by the <u>piano</u> dynamic context. The open
fifths of the piano's right hand that begin the song as con-
sonances close its final measures as further soft dissonances.
These fifths very likely stem from the original string writing,
and their vague, cloudy sound reinforces the poetic portrait
of the past seen through the veil of memory.

Charles Sprague (1791-1875)

Charles Sprague was born in Boston only fifteen years after the founding of the United States, and his family was closely tied to the early history of the nation. His father, Samuel Sprague, was present at the Boston Tea Party. His mother, Joanna Thayer, was a descendant of Peregrine White, the first child to be born to the Mayflower group on this continent. From this illustrious background evolved quite naturally his long, respected career as a Boston banker, while from an early devotion to literature arose his lifelong avocation as a poet. Sprague was evidently a man of some reserve, and the majority of his poems were written not to express personal feelings but to commemorate various public events. Among these were Prologues celebrating the opening of theaters in New York (1821) and Philadelphia (1822), which won the offered prizes and gained him national recognition. Similar occasions and prizes followed, and in 1830 he produced the "Centennial Ode" for the hundredth-anniversary celebration of the settlement of Boston. It is from this tribute to the Pilgrims and to the indigenous peoples they found here that Ives took his text for "The Indians."

Charles Sprague's moving requiem for the natives of America was, in 1830, prophetic of the sufferings they were to endure during the rest of the nineteenth century. When Charles Ives encountered it almost a hundred years later, the subject obviously made a considerable appeal to his strong sense of social justice and his immersion in America's past. He orchestrated it first in 1912 for voice, trumpet, bassoon, piano, Indian drum, and strings, and arranged it in 1921 for voice and piano. In this remarkable song, Ives intended to create a dirge for a lost race, as is clearly indicated by the slow tempo, narrow-range melody, and repetition in both voice and piano parts. Ignoring the damage to the original rhyme scheme, which is no longer pertinent to his musical assimilation of the poetry, Ives omits lines 2, 7, and 8 of this ten-line poem and repeats the key phrase "No more" in measure 7. From the impetus of this repetition, the vocal line begins a keening incantation, which mounts in intensity through carefully placed accents and increased tempo and dynamic levels (see Example 3.13).

Throughout this chant (as in the entire song) measure signatures are constantly changing, syncopations abound, and

Example 3.13, measures 5-8. Copyright © 1957, Associated Music Publishers, Inc.; used by permission.

there are many instances of the kind of misplaced accents on unimportant words that were later to characterize Stravinsky's English-language settings.

Example 3.14, measures 11-13. Copyright © 1957, Associated Music Publishers, Inc.; used by permission.

The dirge-like character of this modified ABA form is also underlined by a repeated chordal pattern in the accompaniment, which is stated alone in the first two measures and many times thereafter behind the voice (primarily in the A section). These chords, which give the effect of melancholy strumming on an ancient folk instrument, also participate in the voice's melodic material. In a very rare instance in his work, Ives repeats the top line of the chordal sequence in canonic imitation for the vocal setting of the last phrase: "Their children go to die." Notice that the chords that accompany this phrase are a stripped down, barer version of the original sequence (which reappears in measures 18-19 exactly as in measures 1-2).

Example 3.15, measures 18-21. Copyright © 1957, Associated Music Publishers, Inc.; used by permission.

Ralph Waldo Emerson (1803-1882)

Ralph Waldo Emerson, perhaps the greatest of all nineteenth-century American men of letters, led a life filled with paradox. He was a mediocre student at Harvard and a minister who left the calling, yet his writing and religious thought were to influence many generations. He knew the darkness of youthful poverty and the deaths of two brothers, his first wife, and young son, yet went on to establish the Concord Transcendentalists, whose belief rested in essential goodness. Finally, although his literary reputation was for many years founded primarily on his essays and the lectures on which they were based, critics are now coming to believe that Emerson's poetry and its influence on the major American poets who followed have both been grossly underrated.[12]

     Despite Emerson's vast importance to the creative life and thought of Charles Ives, it was not primarily as a poet that the composer valued him. In the opening sentence

of "Emerson" (number two of the Essays Before a Sonata[13]),
Ives writes, "It has seemed to the writer that Emerson is
greater ... in the realms of revelation--natural disclosure--
than in those of poetry, philosophy or prophecy. Though a
great poet and prophet he is greater, possibly, as an invader
of the unknown--America's deepest explorer of the spiritual
immensities. "

Interestingly, it is this very aspect of Emerson as
spiritual explorer that places him in the forefront of a char-
acteristically American tradition of poetry. In H. H. Wag-
goner's words, "American poetry has tended ... strongly to-
ward the metaphysical" and "at its best ... has generally
centered its attention on searching out the possibilities of
discovering ultimate meaning in individual experience. "[14]
It is perhaps impossible and certainly unnecessary for our
purposes to delineate the boundary between Emerson the poet
and Emerson the mystic. It is sufficient to observe that the
total impact of the man on Charles Ives is magnificently re-
vealed in the "Emerson" movement from the monumental
Concord Sonata and the essay that precedes it. The song set-
ting called "Duty" is a tiny fragment by comparison, but an
interesting one.

"Duty" was originally composed for male chorus with
orchestra, somewhere between 1911 and 1913, and rescored
for voice and piano in 1921. It forms a pair with a setting
of a Latin text by Manlius called "Vita" (or "Life"). Ives's
original subtitle--"Two slants, or, Christian and Pagan"--
refers to a church sermon heard in Redding, Connecticut,
which was the inspiration for these two songs. The Emer-
son fragment says simply:

> "So nigh is grandeur to our Dust
> So near is God to man,
> When Duty whispers low 'Thou must, '
> The youth replies 'I can. ' "

The Manlius quotation is a single line stating that we are
born to die and our end is implicit in our beginning.

It is easy to see why this sermon would have had
meaning to the optimist and activist Ives, who believed in
religion as a foundation from which every human being might
rise to life's challenges. The source of the Emerson verse
is section III of a poem called "Voluntaries" (a voluntary

being a musical prelude). These particular preludes are trumpet calls to war (in this case the Civil War), for the first two sections mourn the plight of the black in America while the last three importune the youth of the country to heroic action in the slave's behalf.

The setting of "Duty" is the first one of the list to have no meter signature, although all seven measures except the first are in a clear 4/4 or 5/4 grouping. It is also the first to show no repetition in its formal structure, and indeed almost all the songs remaining to be considered will be through-composed. The piano writing incorporates the huge handfuls of dissonant chords covering several octaves that are typical of Ives's orchestral reductions. Frequently these chords are made up of several separate triadic elements, such as the one that occurs on the first syllable of "grandeur" and includes E-flat minor in the bass clef topped by an F major seventh and an open fifth on C-sharp (see Example 3.16).

Even in this short space of seven measures, Ives incorporates many details of word painting in setting the text, which help to make this brief musical moment into a complete dramatic experience. Notice the upward sweep of the melodic line over the word "grandeur" and the literal use of the closest chromatic interval, the half-step, to set "near."

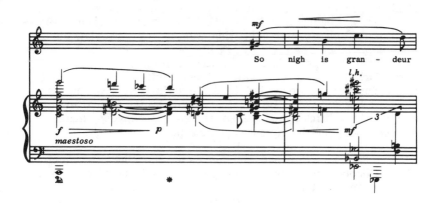

Example 3.16, measures 1-4. Copyright 1933, Merion Music, Inc.; used by permission.

In the second score, Duty's whispering is suggested by very soft portamentos, and the Youth's bold reply is a loud straightforward diatonic cadence, which seems doubly strong after the harmonic and rhythmic confusion that precedes it.

Walt Whitman (1819-1892)

Walt Whitman was not New England born nor was he a product of its historical and intellectual tradition. His father was a Quaker farmer and carpenter, and the family moved to Brooklyn from a Long Island farm when Walt was five years old. Whitman's only formal education was in the Brooklyn public schools, but he read widely on his own and absorbed a great deal from the opera, theaters, and immigrant cultures of New York City. In contrast to those writers who looked toward Europe and were tied to America's past, Whitman's gaze was westward. He was an expansionist in matters geographical, political, and personal, and to express these widened horizons he invented a new poetic language.

        This language had its source in the Old Testament of his childhood and in the Shakespearean and operatic cadences that became so familiar to him as a young man. It was to find its chief object in the glorification of the common people--whom Emerson and Transcendentalism had philosophically applauded but never artistically portrayed.

64

Whitman's debt to Emerson was great, and its true extent is only beginning to be understood.[15] It was no doubt Emerson's concept of a spiritually based, free, original American poet that enabled Whitman to grow into that image. It follows with equal logic that Ives, who shunned the preciousness of the "Rollos"[16] of the world and who described his own spiritual and artistic quest in terms of the aggressive, the masculine, and the homespun, would be drawn to the poetry of Walt Whitman.

Yet although Whitman was indeed one of his favorite poets, Ives set him only once. The song called "Walt Whitman" was originally scored, in 1913, for chorus and orchestra, but the orchestration was vague and sketchy, with the instrumentation indicated toward the end by marginal notes only. In 1921, he rescored it for voice and piano along with a number of others as previously discussed. Given that Ives was to compose only one Whitman setting, this choice of text seems exactly appropriate. It is a pithy, five-line extract from the twentieth section of the most important poem in Whitman's monumental Leaves of Grass. "Walt Whitman" is actually an earlier title of "Song of Myself, " which many critics consider to be Whitman's greatest poem. Indeed, this poem is central to Whitman's celebration of his own mind and body and that of his fellow human beings.

Although there is no formal repetition in this setting, two types of alternating material appear that seem to grow out of the text. The opening challenge of the question and the all-inclusiveness of the answering description is set in a broad, sweeping style whose chromatic melody, big polytonal chords, and nonmetric rhythm create an appropriate sense of freedom and abandon (see Example 3. 17). The next four measures move to a 4/4 meter with a square, almost martial rhythm and simple, diatonic triads using open fifths in the piano's treble clef. One sees this as probably a musical representation of strength, both that specifically referred to in the text and the strength that Ives felt pervaded Whitman's life and art.

Ives makes two small textual omissions from the line that follows, quoted here in the original (underlined words omitted):

"What is a man anyhow?   What am I?   and what are you?"

65

Example 3.17, measures 1-4.   Copyright 1933, Merion Music, Inc.; used by permission.

In setting these three questions, he now combines the two former styles, retaining the heavily accented rhythm but breaking it down into faster-moving eighth notes, whose urgency increases with the returning chromaticism.   Then the quarter-note rhythm comes back, along with the diatonic harmony, now expressed in full four-voiced accompanying chords.   In the extremely interesting final measures, Ives goes from diatonicism to chromaticism to whole-tone scales in an increasingly ambiguous harmonic coloration (see Example 3.18).

It has been pointed out that the tendency to ambiguous endings in Ives's work relates to Realism, a literary movement of the late nineteenth century that attempted to

66

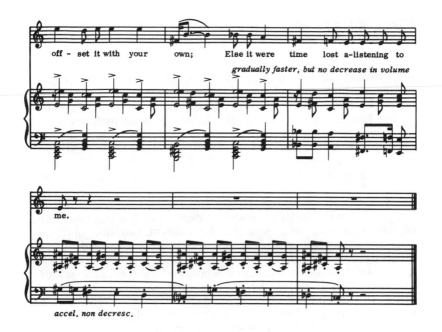

off - set it with your own; Else it were time lost a-listening to

gradually faster, but no decrease in volume

me.

accel. non decresc.

Example 3.18, measures 12-17.   Copyright 1933, Merion Music, Inc.; used by permission.

imitate life.[17] The lifelike suggestion here is that the song has simply stopped, not ended, and it is reinforced by the fact that the dynamic level remains fortissimo, even as the tempo increases to a sudden and unexpected cutoff.

Vachel Lindsay (1879-1931)

_____

Vachel Lindsay is the only poet of this group who was of Midwestern origin.   He was born in Springfield, Illinois, and turned an early desire to be a missionary into a lifelong crusade for the arts in America.   Like William Blake, he was an artist as well as a poet, and in his early poetry shows the influence as well of Poe, Lanier, and Swinburne.   But it is the later Lindsay whom we consider typical: the Lindsay who traveled the country reading such hypnotic verses as "The Congo" and "General Booth" to excited crowds who joined in the chants and perhaps provided the indicated instrumental accompaniments.

Walt Whitman had begun to speak for the common people; Vachel Lindsay brings whole groups of common people before us in living color and action. Although he acknowledged Emerson and Whitman in his "Litany of Heroes, " it is not known exactly how well Lindsay was acquainted with their writings. The vigorous grass-roots attitude clearly derives from Whitman, while the style does not. When an uneven poetic inspiration began to fail him totally, Lindsay tragically ended his own life by drinking poison at the age of fifty-two.

"General William Booth Enters into Heaven" was one of the twenty-odd poems using the four-stress line that Vachel Lindsay read with great effect to college crowds and other groups throughout the United States. He had been moved by Booth's story, as it appeared in the death notices, to create this poem in the rhythm of a Salvation Army hymn. [18] In similar fashion, Charles Ives was moved to set it after reading a few selected lines reprinted in a local newspaper's book-review section in 1914. This is certainly one of Ives's best-known, most extensive, and dramatically effective songs, and some of its aspects have been discussed at length in the Ives literature. [19]

This song is a representation in microcosm of all Ives's major philosophical and musical preoccupations. Here we find again the Realist's imitation of life, this time through the inclusion of a multiplicity of sound materials (instrumental imitations, hymn and song quotations, shouts and screeches), which add up to the evangelist's aural chaos. We also find the various levels of Ives's religious experience and concern, which ranged from revivalism itself to the Transcendental belief in the primacy of the common.

Musically, the Ives trademarks are many, now fully developed and at the same time totally subservient to dramatic ends. Here is the additive structure of one unlike section following another, unified by frequent interpolations of the hymn-tune quotation, which comes into full flower at the end. Here are Ives's dissonant cluster chords utilizing their percussive effect in imitation of Booth's "big bass drum, " and here are the declamatory vocal passages employing many repeated or adjacent tones, which Ives often used to suggest the speech-like quality of his text.

68

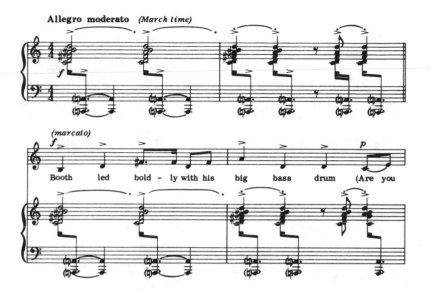

Example 3.19, measures 1-4. Copyright 1935, Merion Music, Inc.; used by permission.

Example 3.20, measures 91-92. Copyright 1935, Merion Music, Inc.; used by permission.

Ives's well-known complexity of rhythmic organization is strongly in evidence throughout this song. One form it assumes is unusual meter signatures and/or unlike adjacent meters.

Another form is that of a complex relationship within a measure between notes and accompaniment (see Example 3.20).

One of the most effective aspects of Ives's setting of "General Booth" arises from his well-developed ability to sense what he needed from a poem and how he must adapt it for his purposes. In this instance, Ives uses thirty-one lines out of fifty-six, or three sections out of seven (sections here being defined as separated by instrumental indications). From the lines chosen, he omits only two words ("the" before "saints" in measure 13 and "there" before "round" in measure 87); he adds only two ("Hallelujah" in measure 10 and "Lord" in measures 62 and 63); and changes only one ("Then" becomes "yet" in measure 91). But it is his constant use of text repetition throughout the setting that in large measure creates the hysterical crescendo of emotion that is the prevailing climate of revivalism. Almost every poetic statement of the refrain "Are you washed in the blood of the lamb?" is repeated by Ives as a whole or in multiple parts.

Example 3. 22, measures 75-81.   Copyright 1935, Merion
Music, Inc.; used by permission.

The phrase "round and round" is repeated four times in a
narrow-range vocal chant that becomes increasingly hypnotic.

Example 3.23, measures 85-90.   Copyright 1935, Merion Music, Inc.; used by permission.

Finally, Ives expands a single "Hallelujah" in the second section to a veritable litany of five "Hallelujahs" and two "Lords" in a frenzy of evangelical ecstasy that is reinforced by the tumbling syncopation and uneven measures (see Example 3.21).

Henry David Thoreau (1817-1862)

Thoreau was another of Ives's New England philosophical mentors of the Transcendental persuasion.   Like Emerson, he was an indifferent scholar at Harvard while receiving a sound classical education there, and he refused Harvard's diploma, claiming that he had "better use for five dollars." During his working lifetime, he was variously engaged as a schoolmaster, manager of his father's pencil factory, and handyman and disciple in the home of Emerson.   The years

1845 and 1847 were spent in the well-known sojourn by Walden Pond, where his true vocations of naturalist and essayist received free rein.

The principal sources of Thoreau's writing were the journals that he kept from 1834 to his untimely death from tuberculosis in 1862. In the early 1840s, he gave up poetry, which had never been a congenial medium, for prose, which was, in his hands, a poetic form. Indeed, the text of "Thoreau" is a quotation adapted and rearranged from the essay in Walden entitled "Sounds," yet the writer finds the inclusion of this song with other settings of American poetry totally appropriate.

The song bears the date of 1915 and comes at the end of Ives's long years of work on the Concord Sonata (1909-1915). [20] Like many of his other songs that were to emerge from instrumental works, this one was adapted from the material of the last movement of the sonata, which was also titled "Thoreau." Both the piano piece and the song are representative of what Hans Nathan calls Ives's "Thoreauesque communion with Nature." This is a theme that runs through much of his music, and by which he is inspired "in particular by the chance simultaneity of heard and seen phenomena such as rustling trees, echoes, mist, and their varigated intensities."[21]

The text is actually divided into two sections, the first of which is printed with the obvious intention of being read aloud by the singer, although it is unfortunately omitted in some performances. These lines are a perfect example of the "simultaneity of heard and seen phenomena" mentioned above, and describe the effect of distance on Thoreau's perceptions at Walden of the Concord bell and of a far-off azure-tinted ridge of earth. For the music played by the piano as background to the reading, Ives draws from the second score of page 63 of the Concord Sonata.[22] He uses chordal material, which he first presents as a harp-like sweep up the keyboard (suggested by the text), then as an alternation of hazy chordal configurations and bell-like tones. This material, like all the rest in this adaptation, is transposed up for the song setting, and in this case is a whole-tone higher than in the sonata (see Example 3.24).

The rest of the text, which is sung by the voice, describes Thoreau lost in his reveries at Walden, and here

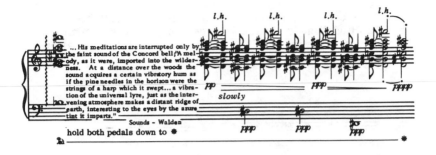

Example 3.24.   Copyright 1933, Merion Music, Inc.; used by permission.

Ives has added to the original material a vocal line that is largely chant-like with many single-note repetitions. He superimposes this line on material that is drawn from page 66, third score, in the sonata (transposed up a half-tone) followed by page 65, third and fourth scores (transposed up a whole-step).

All these elements come together to produce a remarkable effect despite the brevity of this setting. The sense of concentrated, meditative stillness is achieved by the soft dynamic level, the vocal repetition and the ostinato figure in the bass, which perfectly sustains the mood if performed according to Ives's directions ("very slowly and with even rhythm").

Example 3.25.   Copyright 1933, Merion Music, Inc.; used by permission.

75

As a final crowning touch, Ives sets the last syllable of the word "solitude" as a unison between the voice and piano, which creates a very "solitary" effect indeed coming after the preceding mass of blurred, unresolved dissonances.

Example 3.26.   Copyright 1933, Merion Music, Inc.; used by permission.

Louis Untermeyer (1885-1978)

Louis Untermeyer was a New York poet who led a long and distinguished career in American literature.   Besides his volumes of original poetry, he also published translations, paraphrases, and witty imitations of other poets, and is perhaps best known in his capacity as editor of such critical anthologies as Modern American Poetry.[23]

Much of his original poetry is distinguished by an expansive, romantic quality that is certainly apparent in "The Swimmers, " a poem that captured Ives's attention when it appeared in the Yale Review of July 1915. Here again, Ives uses only an eleven-line fragment of the original fifty-eight, but his setting maintains the vigorous, life-intoxicated atmosphere of this moment, when a young man pits his strength against the sea.

This song, like "Thoreau, " is composed essentially without bar-lines. Although some sections do have a clear metric organization, the overall effect is that of a free ranging rhythm in constant response to the ebb and flow of the text. The accompaniment is among Ives's most pianistic and technically demanding. Shades of Chopin are evoked in his opening indication of "Slowly (as a Barcarolle)" and by virtuoso passages of rapid scales and arpeggios, full and broken-chord figures, etc. We know, however, that we are in Ives's world, not Chopin's, not only by the dissonance but also from the Ivesian footnotes. These inform the pianist to play a phrase not precisely the number of times written, or to add an extra player in a very heavily scored section, or to make the suggested variations of the most difficult figurations.

In this type of footnote (similar to those that appear in the song "Charlie Rutlage" and other of his compositions), Ives makes it clear that the precise musical details are less important to him than their contribution to the overall effect. And a highly dramatic effect it is indeed, as the piano imitates the surge and swell of the water, at the same time forming the background and also a kind of adversary to the vocal line, which expresses the poet's struggle to master the sea's natural force.

Against the unconventional aspects of this setting, Ives here again juxtaposes time-honored techniques of word painting in the vocal line. "The swift plunge" is portrayed by a rapid downward rush of three increasingly large intervals (see Example 3. 27). "Swiftly I rose" is an upward chromatic line with a tempo marking of "gradually faster" (see Example 3. 28). "Turbulent strife" and "the feverish intensity of life" are also set with rapidly moving notes and the harmonic urgency of chromatic intervals (see Example 3. 29). The vocal setting of "I lurched and rode the wave" forms an actual picture of the text in its melodic movement of a large leap followed by a gently rocking alternation of whole-steps up and down (see Example 3. 30).

Example 3. 27.   Copyright 1933, Merion Music, Inc.; used
by permission.

Example 3. 28.   Copyright 1933, Merion Music, Inc.; used
by permission.

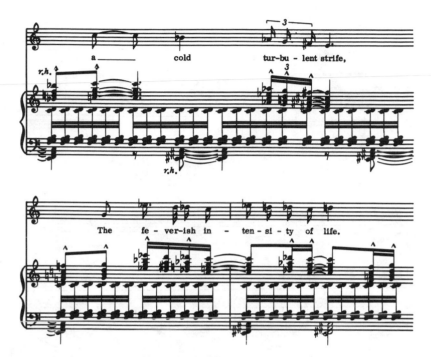

Example 3.29.   Copyright 1933, Merion Music, Inc.; used
by permission.

"Swimming hand over hand" is another pictorial suggestion,
which is heightened by Ives's repetition of "over hand" (see
Example 3.31).

In the final line, the "sea's vain pounding" is sug-
gested by an alternating pattern of accented chords in the
accompaniment, as the piano continues to represent the wa-
ter to the end of the song.   Interestingly, the word "master, "
which connotes the strength and resolution of man triumphing
over nature, is set here with a simple D major diatonic
triad: the only one of its kind in the entire song.   This is
reminiscent of the similar diatonic ending of "Duty" on the
words "I can, " and seems to give the lie to a notion ex-
pressed by some writers that Ives always equated strength
with difficulty and complexity in his music (see Example
3.32).

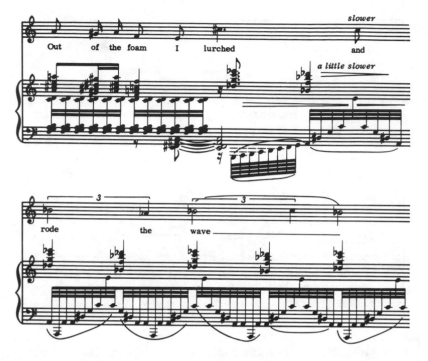

Example 3.30.   Copyright 1933, Merion Music, Inc.; used
by permission.

a - gainst the _ wind; I _ felt _ the sea's _

Example 3.31.　Copyright 1933, Merion Music, Inc.; used
by permission.

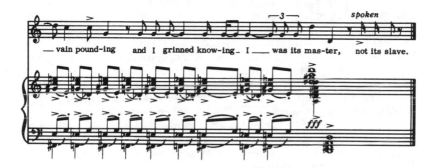

_ vain pound-ing and I grinned know-ing_ I _ was its mas-ter, not its slave.

Example 3.32.　Copyright 1933, Merion Music, Inc.; used
by permission.

James Fenimore Cooper, Jr.　(1892-1918)

World War I was a shock from which Charles Ives and his
faith in human progress never recovered.　In 1918, he had
a serious illness that left him with permanent damage to his
heart, and from 1919 to 1921 his composition was limited to
the solo-song arrangements from former choral or instru-
mental works, and a few new songs.　After 1921, there were
no further completed works, although Ives lived on until 1954.

The Charles Ives of "Afterglow" (1919) and "Maple
Leaves" (1920) is a different man from the Ives of the earlier

81

songs. Gone is the social libertarian's faith in the common people and their destiny, and gone is the joyful Transcendental immersion in the eternal oneness of nature and God. What is left, as expressed in these texts, seems to be an autumnal resignation to the transitory nature of the good and beautiful things of life.

James Fenimore Cooper, Jr., who was born in Albany, New York, was a great-grandson of the novelist, [24] but was unlike his famous forebear in two important ways. Whereas the elder Cooper had been expelled from Yale after two years, the younger not only graduated Phi Beta Kappa from the same institution but received other literary and scholarly honors, and was class secretary as well. Further, where the great-grandfather's early experiments in poetry had revealed his incapacity for the art, the great-grandson showed considerable promise as a poet, a promise that was cut off by his early death.

After leaving Yale, James Fenimore Cooper, Jr., spent several years traveling in Europe and the western United States, and made an unsuccessful attempt to study law at Harvard. He had about decided to settle at Cooperstown, New York (founded by the novelist's father), and pursue a writing career, when World War I drew him into the start of what seemed to be a promising career in the military. However, he caught pneumonia and died at Camp Dix, New Jersey, and the only published collection of his verse appeared in 1918 as a memorial volume.

A few of the poems in this volume (of which "Afterglow" is the frontispiece) had already appeared in the Yale literary magazine, so it is possible that Ives had already known of the young poet's work before the posthumous publication. It is interesting that for both of these late songs Ives chooses very short poems ("Afterglow" is eight lines, "Maple Leaves" four) and sets them just as they are, with no deletions, additions, repetitions, or changes. The style of "Afterglow" is much like that of "Thoreau," with an absence of bar-lines, many widely spaced accompaniment chords made up of superimposed harmonies, and a narrow-range melody of largely stepwise motion. At various points in this stepwise motion, Ives employs two of his favorite nondiatonic forms of organization: the whole-tone scale for the opening phase and the chromatic scale to set "Lingers still the afterglow. "

At   the qui-et close of day,

Example 3. 33.   Copyright 1933, Merion Music, Inc.; used by permission.

low,—— Lin-gers still the— af - ter - glow;

Example 3. 34.   Copyright 1933, Merion Music, Inc.; used by permission.

The song as a whole seems to center around E and its stepwise neighbors (E-flat, D, F, F-sharp) in a technique reminiscent of one Stravinsky was to use heavily in his neo-classic period. [25] The two vocal fragments just quoted center on E and E-flat, respectively, and the close of the song approaches E by the Phrygian lowered second step (see Example 3. 35). Other melodic goals of the vocal line are F and F-sharp, while the piano has many reiterations of E-flat as a low pedal tone (see Example 3. 36).

Word painting does not occur in this song, although the entire setting is a musical expression of such words as

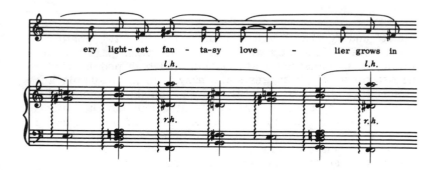

ery   light - est   fan - ta-sy   love -   lier grows in

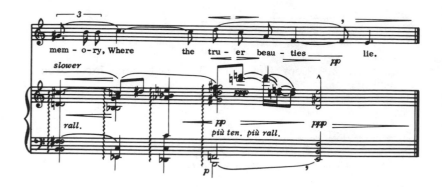

Example 3.35.   Copyright 1933, Merion Music, Inc.; used by permission.

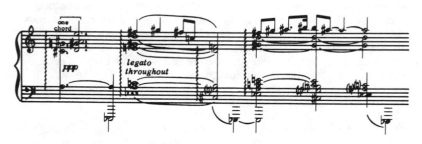

Example 3.36.   Copyright 1933, Merion Music, Inc.; used by permission.

"quiet" and "gently," which occur in the first two poetic
lines.   Ives's footnote, which says "The piano part should
be played as indistinctly as possible and both pedals used
almost constantly," suggests the hazy, almost inaudible aura
of sound he wishes to establish.   The mood that emerges
represents the psychological hush that occurs as the dying of
the light reaches its final moments.   In Griffes's setting of
Lanier's "Evening Song," this same moment is one of love's
joyous confirmation.   By contrast, the dying of the light in
"Afterglow" seems attended by uncertainty and regret.

Thomas Bailey Aldrich (1836-1907)

Thomas Bailey Aldrich, born in Portsmouth, New Hampshire, became a well-known novelist and poet despite the fact that his father's death prevented him from attending Harvard as he had planned. He began his career, as did so many nineteenth-century writers, as a newspaper editor, and also served as correspondent in the Civil War. In 1865, he moved to Boston, and in 1881 took over the editorship of the Atlantic Monthly from William Dean Howells. After 1891, he retired from the Atlantic and devoted his remaining years to writing.

Aldrich's position in literary history is as one of a group of conservatives who, from the Civil War to the turn of the century, tried to hold the line against the materialism of the age and against Realism in literature. His poetry surpassed his prose, and he was a superb craftsman in the poetic art. The "quatrains," or four-line poems, are generally conceded to be among his best poetic statements, and "Maple Leaves" is one of these.

Ives's craftsmanship in this setting is in every way equal to the poet's, and the result is a tiny jewel of a song almost glittering in the brilliant perfection of its eleven measures. The composer now returns to the world of barlines, and the beats add up to 4/4 throughout, although there is no meter signature. Syncopations and unusual accents in the text setting and accompaniment, however, belie the seeming simplicity of the rhythmic organization.

Example 3.37, measures 4-6. Copyright © 1957, Associated Music Publishers, Inc.; used by permission.

The harmony proves deceptive, also, and a simple opening in G major soon begins to "turn" just like the maple leaves. Increasing chromatic additions to voice and piano parts culminate in a most unexpected D-sharp on "gold," and the foreign quality of the harmony portrays the shock of the color transformation.

Example 3.38, measures 1-3. Copyright © 1957, Associated Music Publishers, Inc.; used by permission.

With the second score, a note of the inevitability of loss begins to sound, and Ives matches the text with his melancholy descending vocal line ("The most are gone now"), 26 cloudy harmonies, and faintly insistent repetition of the high B (see Example 3.37).

In measure 7, we realize that this small song is actually a modified ABA form, and it is interesting to note that Ives comes back to the more traditional modes of rhythm and structure in this very late composition. With the return to material like the opening, Ives now expands the chromatic milieu of measures 2 and 3 (Example 3.38). The voice part, as it describes the leaves slipping from the twigs, is a group of short, uneasy half- and whole-step phrases, and in a final portamento series of disappearing half-steps, the leaves cling desperately but vainly to the tree, just as the dying miser tries to hold on to his coins. This is musical pictorialism of great subtlety and power, the more effective in its seeming simplicity.

86

NOTES

1.   This article, called "The Ives Case," was first published in Modern Music in 1934.   In 1940, a few revisions were made and it was republished in Aaron Copland's The New Music (New York: Norton, 1968).

2.   For general discussions of Ives's songs, see: a) H. Wiley Hitchcock, Music in the United States: A Historical Introduction (Englewood Cliffs, New Jersey: Prentice-Hall, 1969), pp. 155-162.   b) H. Wiley Hitchcock, Ives (New York: Oxford University Press, 1977), pp. 9-27.   c) Hans Nathan, "The Modern Period--United States of America," A History of Song, ed. Denis Stevens (New York: Norton, 1960), pp. 431-437.   d) Henry and Sidney Cowell, Charles Ives and His Music (New York: Oxford University Press, 1969), pp. 182-191 and scattered references throughout the text.   e) Rosalie Sandra Perry, Charles Ives and the American Mind (Kent, Ohio: Kent State University Press, 1974), scattered references.   f) John Kirkpatrick, Charles E. Ives--Memos (New York: Norton, 1972), complete listing of all published songs and their reprints to date of publication, pp. 167-177.

3.   The quotation is from Emerson's essay "The American Scholar."

4.   Horatio Parker (1863-1919) was an American composer and educator who chaired the Yale Music Department for twenty-five years.   For a discussion of his influence on Charles Ives, see Perry, p. 9.

5.   Ibid., Chapter II, "Ives and the Transcendental Tradition."

6.   In 1922, Charles Ives had issued a privately printed collection that he called 114 Songs.   Although smaller numbers of these were subsequently reprinted, the collection as a whole went out of print and was only recently reissued in 1975 by Southern Music Co., New York.   All the songs discussed in this chapter, with the exception of "General Booth Enters into Heaven," may be found in the 114 Songs.

7.   By an interesting coincidence, the last of the three girls who appear in stanza 3 ("Grave Alice and laughing Allegra and Edith with golden hair") bore the same name as Charles Ives's adopted daughter.

8. Waggoner, p. 42.

9. There is an earlier anthem version of "The Light That Is Felt" of uncertain date (1895-1902). See Appendix 2, p. 148, and Appendix 4, p. 172, in Kirkpatrick's Memos.

10. Hitchcock, Ives, p. 9.

11. For a further discussion of this hymn and its textual associations, see Hitchcock, Ives, pp. 99 ff.

12. See Waggoner, chapter on Emerson, pp. 90 ff.

13. The Essays Before a Sonata were originally designed to accompany the second piano sonata (or Concord Sonata) but were finally printed separately because of their considerable length. For an extensive treatment of these essays, see Cowell, pp. 81 ff.

14. Waggoner, p. 94.

15. Ibid., pp. 150 ff.

16. "Rollo" was Ives's personification of what he conceived to be a weak, unadventurous, overly traditional approach to the art of music. As an example, see Ives's remarks concerning "Rollo" Henderson (a New York Times music critic) quoted in Kirkpatrick, pp. 30 ff.

17. For a discussion of the influence of Realism on Ives's work, see Perry, pp. 56 ff.

18. General William Booth was the founder of the Salvation Army.

19. Particularly recommended are the treatments in the Hitchcock references listed in no. 2 above. For speculations on the chronology of existing instrumental sketches, see Kirkpatrick, p. 162 and p. 176.

20. The text of the song "Thoreau" was originally embedded in the final chapter of Essays Before a Sonata. Ives printed a small portion of this chapter at the beginning of the "Thoreau" movement of the Concord Sonata. Its use as the song text was, therefore, its third appearance.

21. Nathan, pp. 436 ff.

22.　The page and score numbers given here derive from the Associated Music Publishers' edition of the Concord Sonata. As there are very few bar-lines in the work, measure numbers cannot be supplied.

23.　A conversation between Charles Ives and Louis Untermeyer took place in 1943 or 1944 and is described by Untermeyer in Vivian Perlis's Charles Ives Remembered (New Haven, Connecticut: Yale University Press, 1974), pp. 211-213.　Especially interesting are Untermeyer's speculations as to why Ives set so little contemporary poetry.

24.　In 1905, Harmony Twichell (a graduate nurse since 1900) made a trip to Europe as companion to Mrs. Dean Sage of Albany.　By coincidence, the trip was made in company with J. F. Cooper, the novelist's son, and his son Jimmie, later to become the author of "Afterglow."

25.　Ives's structures in this song resemble the technique (called "pan-diatonicism") in his use of stepwise adjacent tonal centers.　Ives's language, however, is chromatic, whereas Stravinsky's, in this context, was primarily diatonic.

26.　For a revealing anecdote told by John Kirkpatrick about Ives's notation of this vocal fragment, see Perlis, pp. 220-221.

IV.   SETTINGS BY FIVE "AMERICANISTS"

The first two decades of the twentieth century saw the American art song enriched by two diverse strains. On the one hand, there were composers, such as Charles Griffes, whose works incorporated the most sophisticated of foreign influences. On the other, there was Charles Ives, whose secret flowering of astonishingly original songs was largely rooted in native soil. During these twenty years, a new group of composers, all born in the 1890s, was developing. Many of these would follow Ives's lead in turning away from European artistic domination[1] and would become "Americanists, " in Gilbert Chase's terminology. [2] They would explore and incorporate into their serious composition such indigenous American elements as minstrelsy, ragtime and blues, jazz, Negro spirituals, and Anglo-American folk music. [3]

With the passage of half a century, it has become clear that the impulse toward "Americanism" was to a large extent the artistic counterpart of post-World War I isolationism in the political sphere. In truth, most of the five "Americanists" whose songs are about to be discussed did hone their creativity in Europe with Nadia Boulanger. Most of them also experimented at some point with the atonality and serial techniques that were gaining strength as the new European musical language. But the urge to define what was "American" in musical terms was a powerful one to all of them. As the Depression brought the needs of the common people into sharp relief, and the developing mass media made it possible to reach them, these composers labored to find a form of expression that would have meaning to the vast, emerging American musical public.

The songs about to be discussed are by Douglas Moore,
Ernst Bacon, William Grant Still, Roy Harris, and Aaron
Copland. Their dates of composition range from 1928 to
1950. The texts are similar in that they are all by Ameri-
can poets, but they differ inasmuch as these American poets
include male and female, white and black, and personalities
ranging from intellectual recluse to self-educated man of the
people. The musical settings are as varied as their poetic
origins, yet each is a unique embodiment of the "American"
in music: an artistic representation, as it were, of one of
the many faces of America.

Douglas Moore (1893-1969)
Stephen Vincent Benét (1898-1943), Theodore Roethke
(1908-1963)

Few, if any, American composers have equaled Douglas
Moore in number of generations of ancestors in this country.
His father's forebears emigrated from England before 1640
to establish the oldest English-speaking settlement in New
York State at Southold Town on Long Island. His mother
traced her family tree back to Miles Standish and John Al-
den, and Moore's elder daughter reinforced the Puritan
strain by marrying a descendant of Governor Bradford.

The composer himself was born in Cutchogue, Long
Island, and while preparing at Hotchkiss for Yale he met
Archibald MacLeish, a classmate. MacLeish was the first
American poet of the several with whom Douglas Moore was
to establish fruitful collaborations. At Yale, he studied, as
had Charles Ives, with Horatio Parker, and spent two years
beyond the Bachelor of Arts taking a second undergraduate
degree in music. During one of his summer vacations, he
wrote a number of songs while living at the MacDowell Col-
ony, an artistic enterprise to which his family had made
financial contributions. A stint in the U. S. Navy during
World War I led to collaboration with John Jacob Niles on
an amusing volume called Songs My Mother Never Taught Me.
When the war was over, Moore resisted pressure to enter
the family publishing business and went off to Paris to study.
Here he worked with Vincent D'Indy and also with Nadia Bou-
langer, the gifted teacher who helped so many Americans
find their own unique styles of composition.

In Paris, he met Stephen Vincent Benét, who became his second major American literary source. Through the years, Moore set many of his poems, both for solo voice and choral groups. Their association culminated when Benét's short story "The Devil and Daniel Webster" became Douglas Moore's opera of the same name in 1939. Vachel Lindsay, the third major American poetic force in the composer's life, appeared by chance one day in the library of the Cleveland Museum of Art when Moore was employed there as Curator of Music in the early 1920s. Lindsay was the person who opened his perceptions to the beauty and flavor of American life. Indeed, it was this encounter that inspired an orchestral work called "The Pageant of P. T. Barnum"--the first in Moore's long line of compositions based on American themes.

Douglas Moore was woven even more firmly into the fabric of American musical life by means of his long teaching career at Columbia University. Having joined the music faculty in 1926, he held the position of executive director of the department from 1940 to 1962. From this vantage point, he exerted considerable influence on large numbers of teachers, composers, and performers who received their training at Barnard College or Columbia University (including the present author). For a number of years, his course in twentieth-century music was a highlight of the Columbia undergraduate curriculum offerings. He distilled the essence of his classroom lectures into two volumes published ten years apart: Listening to Music (1932)[4] and From Madrigal to Modern Music (1942). [5]

It is easy to see, therefore, how Gilbert Chase's designation of Moore as an "Americanist" came about. It derived first of all from his choices of subject matter in all musical forms. These included the symphonic poem he programmatically titled "Moby Dick, " a setting of Benét's "Ballad of William Sycamore" for voice and chamber orchestra, and most characteristic of all in contemporary minds, The Ballad of Baby Doe--that highly successful opera, produced in 1955, that dealt with the era of silver mining in the West. Reinforcing the literary and historical allusions, moreover, is the musical language developed by the composer, which Aaron Copland found to be highly "evocative of the homely virtues of rural America. " This language, in its "simplicity and unadorned charm" bore no similarity to anything in serious European music, and was the musical counterpart of a regionalism that had found expression somewhat earlier in American literature and painting. [6]

Moore himself delineated his own artistic goals in much the same terms. "The particular ideal which I have been striving to attain," he said, "is to write music which ... will reflect the exciting quality of life, traditions and country which I feel all about me.... If we ... feel romantically inclined, if we like a good tune now and then, ... is it not well for us to admit the fact and try to produce something which we like ourselves?"[7] The great extent to which he succeeded in these aims is noted by all who have studied and written about his music. It has been perhaps most cogently expressed by the conductor Thomas Scherman, who had been his student at Columbia University. "What I ... have ... come to appreciate," writes Scherman, "is Moore's very personal melodic drive, the inherent dramatic variety and contrast in his music, and above all the ingenuous and intoxicating exuberance it exudes."[8]

Stephen Vincent Benét, who wrote the text of the first song to be considered, was, like Douglas Moore, an Easterner, and was born in Bethlehem, Pennsylvania. There is no record of their meeting before Paris, but one is drawn to speculate on how closely their paths might have crossed during the two undergraduate years when they were both at Yale. (Moore graduated in 1917 and Benét in 1919.) Although he died at the early age of 45, Benét contributed during that short span to many literary forms as poet, playwright, radio dramatist, and short-story writer. Not only was his life devoted to writing, but other family members as well rose to literary prominence. His brother, William Rose Benét, and sister-in-law, Elinor Wylie, were both well-known poets, and his wife, Rosemary, to whom he dedicated some of his most sensitive verses, collaborated with him on a number of occasions.

Stephen Vincent Benét's imagination, again like Douglas Moore's, was fired by American heroes and history. His epic poem John Brown's Body won him a Pulitzer Prize in 1928. It quickly became an American classic for its sympathetic portrayal of the ordinary individuals involved in the Civil War. Western Star (1943), which dramatized the journey of the Pilgrims, was the first part of another American epic unfortunately left unfinished at his death. While much of his poetry, particularly the historical portraits, exhibits

94

a sweeping romanticism,[9] the flavor of "Adam Was My Grand-father,"[10] which Douglas Moore set in 1938, is somewhat different.

The original title of the poem was "For All Blasphemers." In it, the speaker boasts of his kinship with Adam's disobedience and Noah's drunkenness, and his attraction to the charms of Lilith. He also knows that his certain destiny will be "gaudy Hell" and the ministrations of "His Worship" (the Devil). The four swaggering verses are full of a kind of frontier irreverence, which acknowledges a strong faith in the Bible but is nevertheless willing to take on the consequences of sin in exchange for present pleasure.

Moore has made only two small alterations in the poem for purposes of his setting. In the second verse, he changes "Past Hell's most shrinking star" to "Beyond a shrinking star," and in the final stanza, "when His Worship takes me up" becomes "then His Worship." The latter is likely a printer's error, since the original is both sensible and grammatical whereas the change is neither.

The rollicking, lusty tone of the poem is perfectly captured by the strongly accented accompaniment of the song, with its overlay in the voice part of heavy syncopation.

Example 4.1, measures 9-14. Copyright 1938, Galaxy Music Corporation; used by permission.

The Lilith verse changes to <u>dolce</u>, which mood is fostered by legato arpeggios in the accompaniment and a melodic line of melting contours.

Example 4.2, measures 59-65. Copyright 1938, Galaxy Music Corporation; used by permission.

     The harmonic style is for the most part simplistically diatonic, but contrast is created by the fact that verses 1 and 4 are in F minor, while 2 and 3 move to C and D-flat major, respectively. There is an interesting chromatic sidestep near the end to B major through its dominant seventh of F-sharp. This seems designed to represent "gaudy Hell" by means of harmonic color (see Example 4.3).

     The second setting by Douglas Moore to be treated here is somewhat similar in musical language but quite different in mood and atmosphere. "Old Song"[11] was written a dozen years later than "Adam" and uses a text by Theodore Roethke.

Example 4.3, measures 92-96. Copyright 1938, Galaxy Music Corporation; used by permission.

Roethke published his remarkable first collection of poetry, Open House, in 1941, and in the ensuing decades has come to be regarded as one of our leading twentieth-century American poets. He was born in Saginaw, Michigan. His childhood impressions were much influenced by his experiences in the greenhouses of his father, who was a flower-grower by profession. In maturity, his poetic style ranged widely between strict and free forms, the lyric and the dramatic, the rational and irrational, the natural and the mystical. Although Roethke's language remains simple,[12] the thought often leans toward the metaphysical. Some of our finest critics have for this reason placed him in our major poetic tradition as defined by Emerson, Whitman, and Dickinson.[13] Theodore Roethke affirms this metaphysical stance by his own characterization of a poem as "part of a hunt, a drive toward God; an effort to break through the barrier of rational experience."[14]

In "Old Song," the sophisticated simplicity of Moore's style is a perfect foil for the economy of Roethke's language, as the poet recounts how he "came to the willow alone" and waited for his true love by the river until "at last the whole dark came down." The poet and the composer seem, as the title suggests, to have created a folk ballad in which the age-old situation of lost love is lamented strophically in direct, uncomplicated terms. The regular rhythmic patterns and mostly diatonic harmonies reinforce this folk-like atmosphere, while the occasional melodic alterations to a lowered third, sixth, or seventh scale degree give it an almost Elizabethan or at least Appalachian flavor. Subtle details, however, reveal the hand of the art song composer, such as the canonic treatment of voice and piano,

Example 4. 4, measures 1-3. Copyright 1950, Carl Fischer, Inc., N.Y.; used by permission.

the pathos of the large melodic leaps,

Example 4. 5, measures 9-13. Copyright 1950, Carl Fischer, Inc., N.Y.; used by permission.

the pictorial suggestion of flowing water in the lefthand of the accompaniment (see Example 4. 6), and the ending that trails off into uncertainty on the dominant with an unresolved circling figure below (see Example 4. 7).

Example 4.6, measures 24-25. Copyright 1950, Carl Fischer, Inc., N.Y.; used by permission.

Example 4.7, measures 39-43. Copyright 1950, Carl Fischer, Inc., N.Y.; used by permission.

Still another level of meaning appears to this writer as inherent in this poem and its setting. It is underlined by the fact that Moore keeps the mode primarily major and the nature imagery, such as a pianistic birdcall, joyfully pastoral,[15] so that the overall mood of the song is peace, rather than pain. Is there then, one wonders, no specific love, and is the poet rather indulging the favorite fantasy of youth in a beautiful natural setting? Or even further, is this Roethke, the metaphysician, telling us that what he is really "waiting" for is that sense of unity with the material and spiritual world that he has elsewhere expressed in these terms: "I lose and find myself in the long water."[16] Many levels of love, it seems, may be suggested here, and the song retains its power on all of them.

99

William Grant Still (1895-1978)
Paul Laurence Dunbar (1872-1906), Langston Hughes
(1902-1967), Arna Bontemps (1902-1973), Countee Cullen
(1903-1946)

In typical American fashion, William Grant Still possessed a
mixed racial heritage, which included Indian, Negro, and
European strains. His parents were both college-trained
teachers, but his father, who had taught music at the Agri-
cultural and Mechanical College of Alabama, died in his son's
infancy. After this, his mother moved from Woodville, Mis-
sissippi, to Little Rock, Arkansas, where she joined the
English faculty of a local high schooL Young William's de-
veloping musicality continued to be fostered by a grandmother
who sang the traditional Negro spirituals and hymns around
the house, and a step-father who bought him the early Red
Seal operatic recordings and took him to concerts and mu-
sical shows.

William's mother, like so many other parents of ar-
tistic children, would have preferred the more "respectable"
profession of medicine for him, but his growing interest in
music drew him to Oberlin, where a scholarship in compo-
sition was specially created for him. Similar grants allowed
him to study with George Chadwick at the New England Con-
servatory and Edgard Varèse in New York. Through these
studies, he became well grounded in the European modes of
composition that prevailed in the first quarter of the century
in the Eastern cultural centers. It is also interesting to note
that Still gained experience playing orchestral instruments and
orchestrating for people like W. C. Handy, Sophie Tucker,
and Paul Whiteman between the Oberlin and New England Con-
servatory years. This gave him the considerable advantage
of being able to think orchestrally in his composition and at
the same time makes all the more remarkable his sensitive
piano writing in the songs, since his keyboard skills were not
very highly developed.

In the article "My Arkansas Boyhood, " the composer
relates that although his works in Varèse's dissonant idiom
brought him critical acclaim, he felt that they did not truly
represent his own musical individuality and decided to adopt
a racial form of expression. "I then made an effort, " he
wrote, "to elevate the folk idiom ... though rarely making
use of actual folk themes. For the most part, I was de-

100

veloping my own themes in the style of the folk."[17] The
song that he composed in 1927 called "Winter's Approach"[18]
is representative of this period.

The text of the song is by Paul Laurence Dunbar, a
late-nineteenth-century poet born in Ohio, where his parents
had settled after escaping slavery in Kentucky. While in
high school in Dayton, Dunbar was already writing for stu-
dent publications. Upon graduation, lacking funds to go on
to law school as he wished, he took a job as an elevator
operator. In 1893, he published one volume of poetry at his
own expense (raising funds by selling copies on the elevator)
and was then aided by friends in the publication of a second.
One of these friends was William Dean Howells, who in 1896
gave him a full-page review in Harper's Weekly, and also
wrote a highly laudatory preface to Dunbar's Lyrics of Lowly
Life. In this preface, Howells has particular praise for the
poems in Negro dialect, which he found to be quite unique
"divinations and reports of what passes in the hearts and
minds of a ... people whose poetry had hitherto been in-
articulately expressed in music but now finds, for the first
time in our tongue, literary interpretation of a very artistic
completeness."[19]

"Winter's Approach, " a poem from the collection
Lyrics of Sunshine and Shadow, tells how "Ol' Brer Rabbit
be a-layin' low, " knowing "dat de wintah time a-comin' "
and that "de huntah man" and his dog are waiting for him
while the hunter's wife gets the skillet ready. The Brer
Rabbit tales are an old tradition in American black folklore
and were originally told in the Gullah dialect of the blacks
who still inhabit the isolated islands off the South Carolina
coast. As Dunbar writes the poem, it is a skillful crystalli-
zation of dialect and rhythmic patterns into an evocative folk
ballad, which draws sympathy for the crafty but beleaguered
rabbit while it understands the realities of the society that
threatens him.

It was quite natural that Still would turn to a Dunbar
text during the period when he was trying to make a racial
statement by means of "elevating the folk idiom. " He uses
the three swinging verses of the poem exactly as they were
written, except that instead of the indicated repetitions of
the line "He know dat de wintah time a-comin', " which fol-
low each couplet, the composer substitutes a knowing little
five-note humming pattern.

* The humming should be decidedly humorous each time it occurs.

Example 4.8, measures 15-17. Copyright © 1928, G. Schirmer, Inc.; used by permission.

This humming refrain, and the instruction that it "should be decidedly humorous each time it occurs" recalls the "walk-around" of black minstrelsy, and indeed this derivation is reinforced by the suggestion of a strummed banjo in the accompaniment figure of the last verse.

Example 4.9, measures 35-36. Copyright © 1928, G. Schirmer, Inc.; used by permission.

Most of the stylistic features, however, derive from ragtime, including the syncopated accents, repeated outlining of simple harmonies in the left hand, and coloristic "blue" notes in both the offbeat chords and melodic line (see Example 4.10).

William Grant Still's other song of 1927, "The Breath

walk an' wait, He walk right by Brer Rab-bit's gate;

Example 4.10, measures 12-14. Copyright © 1928, G. Schirmer, Inc.; used by permission.

of a Rose, "[20] is very different from "Winter's Approach." In it, he forsakes all folk influences and employs the more "universal idiom" that he was now to turn toward, as he said, in the search for "my own individuality as a composer."[21] The text is by Langston Hughes, one of the major black literary figures of the twentieth century. In the two earliest poems to bring him public notice--"The Negro Speaks of Rivers"[22] (1923) and "The Weary Blues" (1925)-- Hughes was already indicating the preoccupation with the sorrows of his race and the literary transmutation of their speech and song that was to characterize much of his work. In "The Breath of a Rose," however, Hughes, like Still, writes not as a black but simply as an American finding his artistic voice. It is a delicate lyric yet full of repressed emotion, comparing the evanescence of love to the perfume of a rose and to other beautiful things in nature that quickly fade or disappear.

Perhaps the most striking element in this setting is its musical color, or timbre. The harmonic structure, which uses chords with many augmented fourths, fifths, and sixths over pedal points drawn from the basic key of B-flat major, is one of the prime contributors to this color. Another is the alternately sonorous and hazily veiled palette of pianistic effects (see Example 4.11). Over this background, a soprano voice has its gentle, repetitive phrases, which become almost rhythmically hypnotic, only to be interrupted by strange little chant-like recitative figures (see Example 4.12). The influence of Debussy, and the Impressionistic use of aural color to portray the visual aspects of natural

Example 4. 11, measures 4-6. Copyright © 1928, G. Schirmer, Inc.; used by permission.

Example 4. 12, measures 10-12. Copyright © 1928, G. Schirmer, Inc.; used by permission.

scenes, certainly comes to mind in this song, but the composer's specific application of the technique is quite fresh, and the result is a uniquely appropriate setting of this text.

Almost twenty years were now to intervene before William Grant Still, in 1945, would compose Songs of Separation, [23] a remarkable cycle that sets the works of five black poets. During these intervening years, Still wrote operas, symphonies, and choral compositions in his new stylistic synthesis but with subjects often linked to the black experience in the New World. These brought him widespread recognition. Besides a long list of commissions, fellowships, and honorary degrees, he received the additional distinction of being the first black to conduct a major symphony orchestra in the United States and to have an opera produced by a leading company. Howard Hanson, an important patron of the rising composer, presented many of his new works at the annual Eastman festival. Still's second marriage, to Verna Arvey, a fine pianist and writer, proved nourishing to both the personal and artistic aspects of his life.

Songs of Separation is a finely structured cycle of five songs recounting stages and emotions connected with "separation"--not that of a black from white society, but rather of a man from the beloved woman who has rejected him. To create this cycle, the composer made selections from the poetry of Arna Bontemps, Philippe de Marcelin, Countee Cullen, and again, as in 1927, Dunbar and Hughes. He then placed these in a dramatic sequence so that together they formed an effective unit in which the protagonist moves through irony, bitterness, and despair to a restorative search for a new love.

Number one, "Idolatry," sets a poem by Arna Bontemps, who was born in Alexandria, Louisiana, and who became a central figure in black literary circles of the mid-twentieth century as a writer, teacher, and editor. Together with Countee Cullen, he worked on the dramatization of the musical St. Louis Woman, which was produced in New York in 1946. He also collaborated with Langston Hughes on the volumes The Poetry of the Negro (1949) and the Book of Negro Folklore (1958). In "Idolatry," the poet tells his lost love that he will set a statue in a shrine to the memory of what they once shared, so that he can journey there and "set an old bell tolling." The vocal style of this song is based on an arioso-type melodic line that varies from expansive contours to narrow-range recitative (see Example 4.13). It sets the tone of the entire cycle, which as a whole shows some operatic influence, as befits its dramatic orientation, but nevertheless retains the compression and intimacy of the art song.

"Poème," the second song, is in French and sets the work of Marcelin, a Haitian composer, so on both counts will not be treated here, as it is outside the scope of this study. Number three is "Parted," a setting of one of Paul

Example 4.13, measures 15-17. Copyright 1949, Leeds
Music Corporation; used by permission.

Laurence Dunbar's poems in literary English. It may well
have been inspired by his own marriage, which ended shortly
after it began in 1899. Dunbar was then to contract tuber-
culosis, which was exacerbated by heavy drinking, and die at
the tragically young age of 34. In this poem, however, he
is not the doomed, deserted Romantic hero but rather a
sophisticated, ironic observer with enough perspective on
human self-deception to conclude the poem in these terms:

> "Tho' I'll confess that I'm no saint,
> I'll swear that she's no martyr. "

William Grant Still sets these crisp and biting verses with a
declamatory, frequently chromatic vocal line and spare,
punctuating chords in the accompaniment.

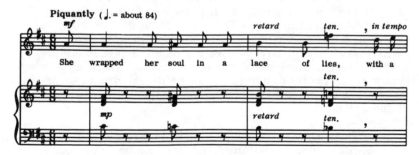

Example 4.14, measures 1-2. Copyright 1949, Leeds Mu-
sic Corporation; used by permission.

This song, which occupies the middle position in the cycle, provides necessary contrast to legato, lyric settings on either side of it.

The fourth poem, "If You Should Go, " is by Countee Cullen, who was born in New York City in 1903. This was only one year after Arna Bontemps's birth, and both men were part of the "Harlem Renaissance" in the 1920s, which saw a flowering of talent among black artists. Cullen was a highly educated, scholarly man who was elected to Phi Beta Kappa while at New York University and who received his M. A. from Harvard in 1926. Although he preferred not to be known as a black poet, but simply as a poet, many of his themes are racial, and he published a great deal in the black journals Crisis and Opportunity. Cullen's poetry has been compared to Keats's by virtue of its lyrical quality, and "If You Should Go" certainly demonstrates this in its tenderly expressed request that his love depart as quietly as "the gently passing day" or a vanished dream.

The composer rises to equal heights of lyricism in this short but exquisite setting. The melodic contour builds inevitably to its climax on "Go quietly. "

Example 4. 15, measures 6-8. Copyright 1949, Leeds Music Corporation; used by permission.

The hazily subdued, repeating chordal patterns that characterize the piano part prepare the appropriate atmosphere for the line "a dream, when done, should leave no trace" (see Example 4. 16). And as final elegant details, Still uses a musical caesura to underline the afterthought quality of the

107

Example 4.16, measure 1. Copyright 1949, Leeds Music Corporation; used by permission.

final phrase, and a melodic supertonic degree on the last note to blur the harmonic and emotional image.

Example 4.17, measures 11-13. Copyright 1949, Leeds Music Corporation; used by permission.

For the last song, "A Black Pierrot," the composer returns to the poetry of Langston Hughes. This time, unlike in "The Breath of a Rose," Hughes is very aware of his color, and in the only "black-oriented" poem of the cycle, he sees himself as a clown with a "once gay colored soul" creeping away into the night, which is also black. The poem and the cycle do not end on this despairing note, however. In this only instance of poetic repetition in the Songs of Separation, Still builds a crescendo of hope on the last two lines:

"I went forth in the morning
To seek a new brown love, "

by repeating the second one twice and the first four times
over a rising melodic sequence.   This builds to a dramatic
peak at the end, with the added lift of the ascending form of
the melodic minor scale.

Example 4. 18, measures 40-43.   Copyright 1949, Leeds Music Corporation; used by permission.

Ernst Bacon (1898-   )
Emily Dickinson (1830-1886)

Ernst Bacon's roots were in the urban Midwest.   He was
born in Chicago in 1898, did undergraduate work at the University
of Chicago, then followed the proverbial "Go West"
dictum by taking an M. A. at the University of California.
His musical path eventually led back to Rochester, New York,
where after studying with Ernest Bloch and the conductor
Eugene Goossens, Bacon won the post of assistant conductor
of the Rochester Opera Company.   Like Douglas Moore, he
also became strongly involved with American university education,
by serving initially as a teacher of piano and theory
and later as director of the School of Music of Syracuse University.

When he was only nineteen, Ernst Bacon had published
the brochure "Our Musical Idiom, "[24] which discussed the

newer harmonic language of the day. His own compositional idiom developed as an individual style that was based on the European traditions as well as more current developments. In the 1940s, Bacon grew interested in American themes and composed, among other larger works, an orchestral suite called From Emily's Diary to words by Emily Dickinson: a poet whom he was to set often in the art song context as well. The Anglo-American folk-song heritage also attracted him very strongly, and in 1941 (the same year as the publication of the songs we are about to consider), he arranged some of these in the collection Along Unpaved Roads.

Ernst Bacon's abiding interest and keen insights into the state of vocal music in this country are evidenced in the chapter called "The Singer," which appeared in his Words on Music of 1960. [25] While deploring the decline of the solo song recital and particularly the neglect of our own language in favor of European settings, he nevertheless maintains that " it is quite possible that some of the best musical writing in America has taken the form of song. "[26] He goes on to say that "in America we have a wealth of lyric poetry calling for song, particularly the contributions of the women, beginning with Emily Dickinson. "[27]

It is certainly true that the poems of Emily Dickinson have been exerting an ever-growing fascination on American composers, especially since the publication of the increasingly authentic editions. The romantic life story of the recluse dressed in white, who for twenty years collected her small packets of verse in the seclusion of her Amherst home, would draw our attention even without the towering genius of the poetry. Her gifts, however, are tellingly described by H. H. Waggoner: "If one were forced to choose just one poet to illuminate the nature and quality of American poetry as a whole, to define its ... preoccupations, its characteristic themes and images, its diction and style ... one ought to choose Dickinson. "[28]

Emily Dickinson, like Douglas Moore, was descended from many generations of American ancestors. The first of these sailed to the New World in 1630 and established the town of Hadley, Massachusetts. Later descendants crossed the Connecticut River to found the city of Amherst, where Emily was born in 1830. Her father was a prominent lawyer and legislator, and her girlhood and youth were actively occupied with education and the society of siblings and friends.

Trips to Worcester and Boston were common, and she visited Washington in 1854 during her father's Congressional term.

The first of the two Bacon songs to be discussed, "It's all I have to bring, "[29] sets a fairly early poem written in 1858, when the joy of living was still strong in the writer's consciousness and before coming tragedies had begun to cast their shadows. The text of this song is drawn from the 1929 collection Further Poems, edited by Emily's niece, Martha Dickinson Bianchi, who had also issued another collection, The Single Hound, in 1914. These two editions contained very few alterations, but some misreadings. On the other hand, the approximately five hundred Dickinson poems previously published in the 1890s as transcribed by Mabel Loomis Todd (wife of an Amherst professor) had been "corrected" by Thomas Wentworth Higginson, the editor who had given Dickinson encouragement but little comprehension through the years of her writing. Even the Bianchi versions, however, were to be superseded by Thomas H. Johnson's first actual scholarly edition of all the poetry in an unreconstructed text published by Harvard University in 1955. In this last edition of "It's all I have to bring, " a change of a single letter alters the meaning of the sixth line. In the Bacon song, it reads "Someone the sun could tell" whereas in the original, as edited by Johnson, it is "Someone the sum could tell. "

In either case, the basic feeling of the poem remains the same. The atmosphere is clearly pastoral and filled with the images of fields, meadows, bees, and clover. The mood remains "sunny" even with the loss of the actual word in the definitive edition. The B-flat major key establishes all this, as do the essentially diatonic harmonies, broken only by the accidentals that pictorially surround the word "bees. "

Example 4.19, measures 22-25. Copyright © 1944, G. Schirmer, Inc.; used by permission.

The melodic line participates in establishing the atmosphere by means of long, smooth legato phrases, punctuated by occasional joyous leaps (see Example 4.19).

The "common meter" of Emily Dickinson's verses, which she adapted from hymns because she felt its simplicity suggested life rather than "Literature," is transformed here into a straightforward 2/4 time signature. The addition of an occasional 3/4 bar, however, lends a subtle touch to the musical rhythm, which hints at the tremendous sophistication underlying the apparent simplicity of all Dickinson's poetry.

Example 4.20, measures 1-4. Copyright © 1944, G. Schirmer, Inc.; used by permission.

One is, in fact, led to speculate as to whether an urge toward simplicity is not perhaps a characteristic trait of American art in all forms, as a reaction, possibly, against the increasing complexities with which Europe had come to express its older and less vigorous cultures. Holding this thought in abeyance until a later time, we come now to the second Bacon song called "And this of all my hopes,"[30] which sets a poem dating from 1864. By this time, personal crises and the loss of probably the greatest love object of Emily Dickinson's life, the mysterious Reverend Wadsworth, had begun to be reflected in her poetry, which speaks increasingly of pain and limitation. Pulling away from her early Emersonian belief in transcendental goodness, she began to find "God faceless and nature silent."[31] The poem, then, describes the "silent end" of hope and the early decline of the "bountiful colored morning" of her life.

Its contrasting setting employs a minor key and more dissonant harmonies. The narrower melodic line takes on a crawling, chromatic contour to portray the "confident worm" boring at the roots of her being.

Nev - er a worm so con - fi - dent___

Bored at so brave___ a __ root.

Example 4.21, measures 17-20. Copyright © 1944, G. Schirmer, Inc.; used by permission.

The dotted rhythms and little running groups of sixteenth notes contribute a nervous, unsettling quality (see Example 4.21), and all elements join in a telling musical portrait of gentle despair.

Roy Harris (1898-1979)
Carl Sandburg (1878-1967)

The legendary quality of Roy Harris's "Americanism" began with his birth in a log cabin in Lincoln County, Oklahoma. Although his parents, who were of Irish and Scottish descent,

113

had been early settlers in that state, in 1903 they succumbed to the lure of the golden Pacific coast and moved to California. Harris attended the University of California in 1919 and 1920 as a special student in philosophy and economics, but his musical studies were conducted privately. An important influence in later musical directions was his first major composition teacher, Arthur Farwell, who had been an early champion of new American music and had founded the Wa-Wan Press in 1901.

After Harris's work attracted the attention of Howard Hanson at Eastman, the young composer made the reverse geographical pilgrimage and spent the late twenties absorbing Eastern influences. After working for a time at the Mac-Dowell Colony, he was able, with the aid of several fellowships, to go to Paris, where Nadia Boulanger sharpened and refined his as-yet-undisciplined talent. Back in the United States, he began a long, fruitful career as composer-in-residence and teacher at colleges and universities in many areas of the country.

Roy Harris was very articulate about his aims as a composer and tried to establish verbal equations between the American character and American music. In an essay published in 1933, he developed the theory that Americans have different rhythmic impulses than Europeans, that they lean toward modality to avoid the clichés of major and minor, and that they avoid cadential definition because of an aversion to anything final. [32] All of these elements are brought into play in the song we shall examine, as well as the melodic gift that Aaron Copland found to be Harris's most striking characteristic. As regards Harris's overall style, Copland felt "its American quality strongly. " He perceived it as "music of real sweep and breadth with power and emotional depth such as only a generously built country could produce. "[33]

Interestingly enough, whereas Harris was a prolific composer of instrumental works, he wrote no operas and very few songs. The combining of music with words seemed to have little appeal for him, although he did compose a number of choral works based on the poetry of Walt Whitman, whom he looked upon as a kindred spirit. He felt, in fact, that he had tried to do for music what Whitman had done in poetry. It was therefore not surprising that for the text of the one important art song that Harris contributed to the American repertoire he turned to a poem by Carl Sandburg,

who more than any other writer had taken on the stylistic
and conceptual heritage of Whitman.

This heritage is aptly described by Babette Deutsch,
who characterizes Sandburg's contribution to American poetry
as "a renewed awareness of ordinary life as of ordinary lan-
guage, including slang as poetic diction of a fresh sort."[34]
Born in Galesburg, Illinois, to poor Swedish immigrants--
his mother was a chambermaid and his father a blacksmith
who could not write--Carl Sandburg was well equipped to be
the poet of the common people. His lifelong sympathy for
the oppressed and exploited was expressed politically by his
populism and his labors in behalf of social reform. His
artistic need to express the American experience took many
forms, which included performing and collecting folk songs
all over the country, and literary triumphs ranging from the
prose of the famous Lincoln biography to the many rich col-
lections of poetry.

Despite the fact that he spent the last twenty-two years
of his life at Flat Rock, North Carolina, it is essential to
remember that Sandburg spent his formative years in the Mid-
west with such great creative contemporaries as Theodore
Dreiser, Sinclair Lewis, and Sherwood Anderson. This
enormous Midwestern vitality dominated the American liter-
ary scene between the two World Wars, after which it passed
on to the South. Sandburg was already becoming a part of
this scene by virtue of his writing for newspapers in Milwau-
kee and Chicago, when in 1916 his reputation was firmly es-
tablished with the publication of Chicago Poems.

"Fog,"[35] which forms the text of Roy Harris's song,
is perhaps the most famous poem of that collection. It has
often been cited as a prime example of the "Imagist" approach
to poetry, since its brief six lines personify the fog creeping
over the city as a silent animal that comes and goes on "lit-
tle cat feet." Although short, the poem embodies Sandburg's
basically unmetered, unrhymed, "nonpoetic" style derived
from common speech. Its similarly nonpoetic content, which
paints a rather dreary urban scene, reminds us that Sand-
burg was a contemporary of the "Ashcan" school of Ameri-
can painters.

Harris opens the song with a five-measure piano in-
troduction in which Impressionistic use of the soft pedal for
color and the sostenuto to sustain a D-flat pedal point im-
mediately create the desired "misty" effect.

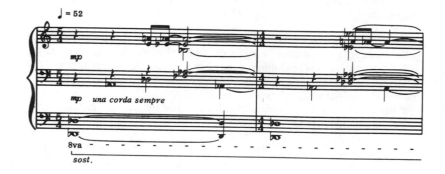

Example 4.22, measures 1-2.   Copyright 1948, Carl Fischer, Inc.; used by permission.

The composer's penchant for polytonality comes to the fore in his superimposition of D-flat major and D minor harmonies,

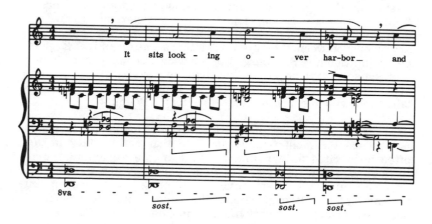

Example 4.23, measures 12-15.   Copyright 1948, Carl Fischer, Inc.; used by permission.

and his modal tendencies are reflected in the melodic setting of "It sits looking over harbor," which also pulls into a pictorial rising curve (see Example 4.23).

Both the modality and polytonality, expressed as they are at a very soft dynamic level, contribute to a harmonic blur. This lack of aural definition is reinforced rhythmically by the subtle, shifting quality lent by the interpolated 5/4 measures embedded in a basically 4/4 meter (see Example 4.22). The end of the song, which is suspended on the uncertain sixth degree of the scalar harmony, is a perfect example of Harris's theory of American avoidance of the final. In his portrait, the fog drifts slowly away, as gradually and silently as it had come.

Example 4.24, measures 24-27. Copyright 1948, Carl Fischer, Inc.; used by permission.

Aaron Copland (1900-   )
Emily Dickinson (1830-1886)

Having been drawn increasingly westward by the origins of Still, Bacon, and Harris, we return, with our final "Americanist, " to the New York area. Unlike Douglas Moore, with his seventeenth-century ancestors, however, Aaron Copland was born in Brooklyn to parents who were Russian Jewish immigrants. Having discovered the art of music on his own, the young Copland studied harmony with Ruben Goldmark, who was also George Gershwin's teacher. After high school, he decided to concentrate totally on music rather than seek a college education and in 1921 enrolled at the Fontainebleau school as the first of the many Americans to study composition with Nadia Boulanger. Here he would shortly meet Douglas Moore, as later in the decade he was to encounter

Roy Harris at the MacDowell Colony; and here his personal style would begin to crystallize by exposure to what Copland saw as Boulanger's "critical perspicacity, encyclopedic knowledge of music and ability to inspire the pupil with confidence in his own creative powers."[36]

Copland had early been drawn to Debussy and Ravel, and continued while in Paris to expand this creative affinity for the French tradition through his studies of Stravinsky, the Gallicized Russian. In 1971, in conversation with Edward Cone, he expressed his admiration of Fauré and revealed that he had never been comfortable with German chromaticism, even in serial form.[37] By the time he left Paris, however, a preoccupation with seeking an American musical identity was already growing among the Boulanger students. "We wanted," says Copland, "to find a music that would speak of universal things in the vernacular of American speech rhythms ... music with a largeness of utterance wholly representative of the country that Whitman had envisaged."[38]

Copland, from the early days of his career, thus became not only one of his country's finest composers, but also, in Irving Lowens's words, "one of our most lucid thinkers and writers about the art"[39] and a great interpreter and champion of the works of others. He has been a moving spirit and organizer of many groups that have promoted new American music, such as the Copland-Sessions concerts of 1928 to 1931, the first American Festival of Contemporary Music at Yaddo (1932), and the American Composers' Alliance. It was, in fact, at the Yaddo Festival that the famous performance of seven songs by Charles Ives occurred, which together with Copland's article on the 114 Songs proved to be the opening wedge in public recognition of Ives's genius.[40]

During the thirties and forties, Copland was much occupied with reaching as broad an American public as possible through the new media of radio, cinema, and phonograph. This is the era of the "big ballets" and a style that eschews former complexities in favor of folk-influenced melodies and rhythms. By 1950, however, the year during which he labored over the monumental Twelve Poems of Emily Dickinson,[41] a new synthesis had already emerged. In it were incorporated the jagged, leaping melodic lines, diatonic dissonances and rhythmic ingenuity that had become the distillation of Copland's search for an American musical aesthetic.

Since it was such a major addition to the American art song literature, and by a composer who had previously been known mostly for his instrumental works, the cycle attracted a great deal of comment in print during the dozen years that followed its publication. Critical barbs, such as Hans Nathan's judgment of unconvincing text interpretation[42] and Joseph Kerman's dissatisfaction with some of the chord construction,[43] were the exceptions. The overwhelming majority opinion, including this writer's, aligned itself with William Flanagan's citing of the work as "probably the most important single contribution toward an American art song literature that we have to date." With a composer's intimate appreciation of another's genius, Flanagan, who himself wrote many fine songs before his tragic death, praised its surpassing originality, varied emotional range, and a "vocal-instrumental fusion which ... is one of the most satisfactory in any contemporary music."[44]

The poems chosen by Copland for these settings cover a twenty-five-year span of Emily Dickinson's life, the earliest dating from 1858 and the latest from 1883. The composer tells us in a brief foreword that they all treat subject matter particularly close to the poet ("nature, death, life, eternity") and that he has attempted to give to the collection the aspect of a song cycle, a musical counterpart of Dickinson's personality. The texts are all drawn from the Collected Poems, which had been edited in 1937 by Bianchi and Hampson.[45] That some of them were corrupt versions became evident in 1955 with Johnson's scholarly edition, but this fact has had very little effect, if any, on the overall impact of the work.

Copland, himself, relates that "The Chariot," which became the final song, was the first Dickinson poem that he was inspired to set. Having first been captured by the visual image it evokes of Dickinson as the bride and Death as the groom, he was then drawn to one after another of her poems, until finally there were a dozen settings. Interestingly, "The Chariot" was the only song of the twelve to which Copland gave his own title, choosing an evocative word that does not appear in the poem itself. For the rest, he, like Ernst Bacon, simply used the first lines of the poems, since the author had never seen fit to lay the burdensome dignity of titles on her verses.

The composer has read and thought a great deal about

the introverted and intellectual aspects of Emily Dickinson's
nature and admits his fascination with the notion that one day
she simply "went upstairs and never came down." He sees
the cycle as needing to be performed by a woman, and the
poems interpreted as she would have interpreted them, "with
a twinkle in the eye" and a very knowing manner. He con-
siders a mezzo-soprano voice to be the most appropriate and
prefers one that is capable of great drama, although through
much of the cycle he thinks of the singer as "talking the
poetry."46

The first song is a setting of "Nature, the gentlest
mother," a fairly early poem (1863), in which Nature is
seen as a mother patiently and tenderly caring for her crea-
tures, overseeing their prayers and silencing the earth while
they sleep. In one of the final lines,

> "With infinite affection
> And infiniter care"

the use of the seldom-seen comparative "infiniter" lends a
retrospectively childlike quality to the whole poem, and this
sophisticated innocence is one of Emily Dickinson's aspects
that Copland emphasizes throughout the cycle by his poetic
choices and musical treatments.

In this setting, he has used a careful definition of the
vocal and pianistic material to delineate his characters and
allow for a wonderful interplay between them. While the
vocal line carries the warm, smooth, slower-moving con-
tours of Mother Nature, the pianistic counterpoint uses rapid,
pictorial figures to suggest the birds, squirrels, and crickets
of her domain.

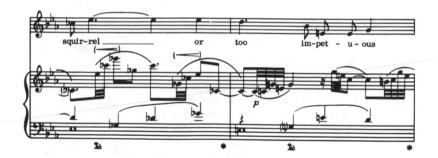

Example 4.25, measures 22-26. Copyright 1951, Boosey and Hawkes, Inc.; used by permission.

The sundown prayers of her children grow to a crescendo of humming crickets and bee-laden flowers

Example 4.26, measures 40-44. Copyright 1951, Boosey and Hawkes, Inc.; used by permission.

before silence is imposed. Copland's thickly sprinkled instructions for alterations in tempo, which appear throughout the cycle, indicate his sensitivity to the changing mood of the text and take full advantage of the greater flexibility of musical rhythm over its poetic counterpart.

Number two, "There came a wind like a bugle," presents a total contrast to the opening mood. This frightening picture of a violent storm was written in 1883, only three years before the poet's death, and the presence of such words as "chill," "doom," and "ghost" may well indicate a subconscious connection in her mind between the menacing storm and approaching, implacable death. Copland's musical imagery here, beginning with a percussive pianistic upward sweep of a scale in parallel sevenths, employs the resources of polytonality, dissonant harmonies, and angular vocal leaps to create a sense of turmoil and terror. Even more specific images include the piano trill that imitates the buzz of the "electric moccasin";

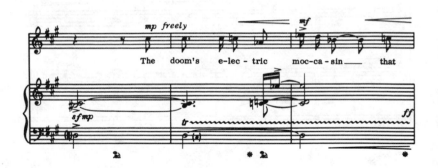

Example 4.27, measures 22-24. Copyright 1951, Boosey and Hawkes, Inc.; used by permission.

the rapid, blurred fourths reminiscent of Schubertian "river" figures (see Example 4.28); and the steeple bell that tolls in the left hand of the accompaniment (see Example 4.29). Vocal color also contributes a great deal, as the many low chest tones called for suggest the brooding "doom" of the poem.

In the third song, "Why do they shut me out of Heaven?," we find the only instance in the cycle of prolonged

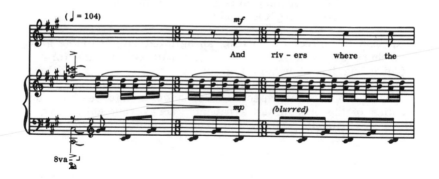

Example 4.28, measures 34-36. Copyright 1951, Boosey
and Hawkes, Inc.; used by permission.

Example 4.29, measures 40-42. Copyright 1951, Boosey
and Hawkes, Inc.; used by permission.

use of recitative-type setting. By this device, Copland in-
dicates that, in the opening and closing lines, he is empha-
sizing the sense of the poetry being spoken. In the author's
opinion, Copland's music serves in this setting not only to
enhance but to add meaning. The text of the 1861 poem is
a rather wistful plea to the angels not to shut the door of
Heaven because of the clamor of the poet's praises. Cop-
land, however, repeats the lines "Don't shut the door" and
"Could I forbid?" and, furthermore, brings back the opening
two at the end of the song:

"Why do they shut me out of Heaven?
Did I sing too loud?"

This has the effect of creating an agitated, importuning atmosphere that almost makes one sympathize with the forbidding angels.   Further, the setting of "Did I sing too loud?" with its double-<u>forte</u> dynamic and large upward leaps (the second time to an unexpected dissonance) reinforces the suggestion of the speaker as a naughty, irreverent child, and attests to Copland's skill in the area of musical humor.

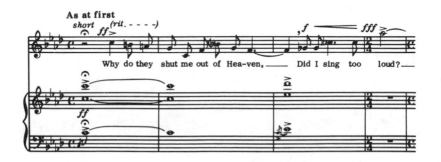

Example 4.30, measures 27-30.   Copyright 1951, Boosey and Hawkes, Inc.; used by permission.

"The world feels dusty," number four, is an inspired musical conception of a poem that states briefly and beautifully that love eases the moment of dying.   Copland has here used a simple rhythmic piano motif (a quarter note followed by a half note), expressed in changing harmonies and dynamics and repeated throughout the song.   The repetition provides both a feeling of the inevitability of death and of the sinking of the dying consciousness into a trance-like state. Over this, a finely contoured, lyric vocal line expresses the caring and compassion of the loving observer (see Example 4.31).

The text of number five, "Heart, we will forget him," comes from one of the earliest poems of the set (1858).   It is the only "love" poem of the cycle, and Copland no doubt chose it to exemplify the part of Emily Dickinson's nature that had been deeply drawn to a man whom she felt she must put out of her thoughts.   There are many who agree with the

Example 4.31, measures 1-5.   Copyright 1951, Boosey and
Hawkes, Inc.; used by permission.

anonymous British critic in Music Review who wrote that
"this song is as exquisitely touching as any that has come
out of America.   Indeed, " he continued, "I have a feeling
that it may be the most affecting song written since Mahler's
death."47

In the two brief verses, the poet exhorts her heart to
join her in forgetting "his" warmth and light, and to hurry,
lest in the meantime she become swept by memory.   The
two elements that make Copland's setting so moving are
first, the pathos of the melodic intervals, and secondly the
use of constantly changing tempi to indicate the speaker's
ambivalence.   With the first marking ("very slowly--dragging"),
the composer suggests that she is really loath to forget him,
but is trying to act determined ("moving forward").

Example 4.32, measures 1-6.   Copyright 1951, Boosey and
Hawkes, Inc.; used by permission.

125

In the subsequent monologue, a sense of growing desperation
is achieved by an accelerando,

Example 4.33, measures 24-27.   Copyright 1951, Boosey
and Hawkes, Inc.; used by permission.

after which a flood of memory slows the musical motion to
a halt.   This is further emphasized by the caesura before
"him."

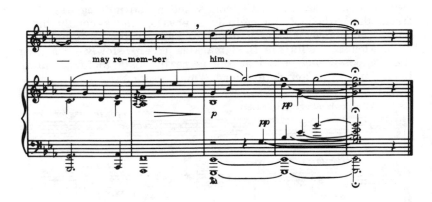

Example 4.34, measures 32-36.   Copyright 1951, Boosey
and Hawkes, Inc.; used by permission.

"Dear March, come in" (1874) follows with an ani-
mated treatment of Dickinson's whimsical conversation with

the personified month. The effect of lively chatter is cre-
ated by the tempo, 6/8 meter, and juxtaposition of a duple
rhythm over the basic quarter-note/eighth-note, quarter-note/
eighth-note pattern. The changes of key are integral in por-
traying the various stages of the visit, the first one mirror-
ing a change of place ("come right upstairs") as the melodic
line pictorially ascends.

Example 4.35, measures 32-35. Copyright 1951, Boosey
and Hawkes, Inc.; used by permission.

The second key change marks the arrival of April, whose
knock is also heard in the left hand of the piano part (see
Example 4.36). The final return to the opening F-sharp
major brings back the initial joy of March's arrival.

"Sleep is supposed to be," number seven, begins
with the opening motive of "The Chariot." Since the latter
was Copland's first setting, the motive's appearance here
in number seven is actually the quotation, rather than vice

Example 4.36, measures 76-81. Copyright 1951, Boosey
and Hawkes, Inc.; used by permission.

versa, and lets us know that this song also is about death
(which is called "sleep" by "souls of sanity"). Emily Dickin-
son's "morning" in this metaphor stands for Resurrection,
and Copland clothes this idea with a "wake-the-dead" phrase--
the highest and loudest of the entire cycle. Reinforcing the
vocal line is a polytonal harmonic construction that suggests
the all-inclusiveness of "Eternity. "

Example 4.37, measures 31-32. Copyright 1951, Boosey
and Hawkes, Inc.; used by permission.

          In many respects, the next song, "When they come
back, " typifies the entire work. Inspired by the conciseness
and precision of language with which Emily Dickinson has

128

stated the ancient fear that spring might not return, Copland has brought to bear the spareness and linear clarity that are hallmarks of his style on one of the cycle's most outstanding settings. Although the composer sees the performing style of number eight as "musing" and displaying "little emotion as though there were no audience, "[48] the tempo indication ("gradually faster") seems to suggest a rising tide of anxiety.

Example 4.38, measures 5-12. Copyright 1951, Boosey and Hawkes, Inc.; used by permission.

This breathless quality is intensified by the closeness of the canonic imitation that occurs off and on throughout the song, always beginning in the piano part and followed by the voice at the interval of only a single quarter note (see Example 4.38).

"I felt a funeral in my brain, " which is perhaps the most dramatic setting of the twelve, is the second instance in the cycle of the composer electing to repeat parts of the text for added emphasis. In this frightening description of

the poet imagining her own funeral, Copland adds an extra
"treading"

Example 4.39, measures 10-13. Copyright 1951, Boosey
and Hawkes, Inc.; used by permission.

and an extra "beating"

Example 4.40, measures 23-25. Copyright 1951, Boosey
and Hawkes, Inc.; used by permission.

to increase the hypnotic terror of the vision. An apt evoca-
tion of the musical macabre, vaguely reminiscent of Ber-
lioz's "March to the Scaffold" in Symphonie Fantastique, is
produced by the inexorable polytonal marching figures of the
opening

Example 4.41, measures 1-3. Copyright 1951, Boosey and
Hawkes, Inc.; used by permission.

and the thudding drum imitations in the pianist's left hand, as
the "service" begins.

Example 4.42, measures 18-22. Copyright 1951, Boosey and
Hawkes, Inc.; used by permission.

      After the "tolling of space" is portrayed, once again,
by a piano figure, the eerie ending softens and slows down
as though to express the emotion of a final verse that appears
in the Thomas H. Johnson version but not in the 1937 one
that Copland had available:

> "And then a Plank in Reason broke
> And I dropped down and down ---
> And hit a World at every plunge,
> And Finished Knowing then ---"

Number ten, "I've heard an organ talk sometimes, "
gives Copland another opportunity to exercise his musical
irony, as the poet speaks of the unconscious influences that
were brought to bear on her by the church services of her
girlhood. In this setting, the harmonies and voicing of the
piano part are like a parody of musically unsophisticated
church music, and the final vocal phrase, which Copland
wanted to have a "fat" sound, [49] recalls the fundamentalist
fervor that Ives builds to dizzying heights in "General Wil-
liam Booth Enters into Heaven. "

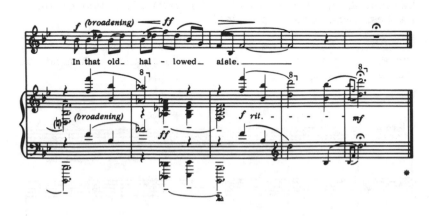

Example 4. 43, measures 31-35. Copyright 1951, Boosey and
Hawkes, Inc. ; used by permission.

    The poem "Going to Heaven" was written in 1859, a
year before "I've heard an organ talk sometimes. " Here
again, we see Emily Dickinson struggling with the realization
that most of the tenets of her early religious teachings are
no longer acceptable to her mind. This time, the tone is
again a mocking one, and Copland makes this clear with his
playful vocal repetitions of the phrase "Going to Heaven, "
which occurs only twice in the poem as opposed to seven
times in the setting (see Example 4. 44).

    The tongue-in-cheek atmosphere that Copland in-
tended[50] is induced by various pianistic comments, such as
rapid imitative figures, rhythmic hemiolas, and gently tit-
tering staccato passages. In the final verse of the poem,
Dickinson confesses that although she herself doesn't believe

132

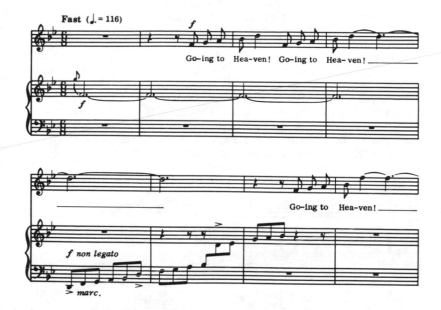

Example 4.44, measures 1-8.   Copyright 1951, Boosey and
Hawkes, Inc.; used by permission.

in Heaven, she's glad that her two loved ones now dead had
had their belief for consolation.   Copland sets these more
serious statements with an augmentation of the vocal rhythm
to dotted quarter notes, but cannot resist a final snickering
reference to the "Going to Heaven" theme, which is briefly
and softly quoted by the piano.

Example 4.45, measures 123-126.   Copyright 1951, Boosey
and Hawkes, Inc.; used by permission.

Last of the twelve is "The Chariot," which, as we have seen, was the original, motivating creative impulse from which the others grew. The opening tempo indication, "With quiet grace," captures the tone of mid-Victorian politeness in which Dickinson unfolds the tale of Death stopping for her in his chariot and driving her past the receding material world to the "swelling of the ground" (i.e., the grave) and thereby, eternity. This whole setting is based on the dotted rhythmic figures, which represent the motion of the horse-drawn chariot. Copland even makes the vocal rhythm conform to this, against the natural word accent, as if to attest to the invincible power of Death.

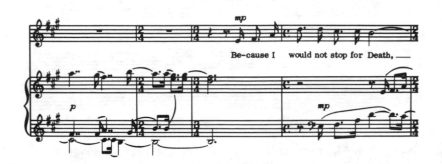

Example 4.46, measures 4-7. Copyright 1951, Boosey and Hawkes, Inc.; used by permission.

As the soul widens out in Death to join with the universal, so does the melodic contour extend to the octave leap of "We passed" and the harmony broaden to a warm B major color for "the setting sun."

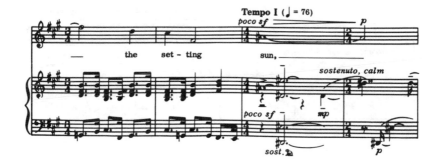

Example 4.47, measures 30-36.   Copyright 1951, Boosey
and Hawkes, Inc.; used by permission.

The dotted-note rhythm begins to slow, then stops al-
together.   Now only brief quotations of the figure bring
memories of the passage into the new state, which took place
"centuries" ago.

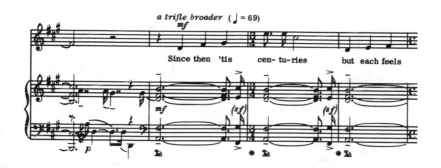

Example 4.48, measures 44-47.   Copyright 1951, Boosey
and Hawkes, Inc.; used by permission.

"Toward eternity" is again set vocally in a dotted figure but
this time in augmentation.   The slower vocal motion sug-
gests that the chariot ride of death (recalled by a piano quo-
tation of the opening motive) was a temporary passage to
the calm of the everlasting.

Example 4. 49, measures 52-56. Copyright 1951, Boosey
and Hawkes, Inc.; used by permission.

In the Brooklyn College address mentioned above (see
note 39), Aaron Copland stressed that it is up to the artist
to affirm the importance of the individual and to express the
essence of the age in permanent form.   He could have chosen
no better candidate to aid him in the affirmation of the indi-
vidual than the Amherst recluse, who, like Charles Ives,
gained expressive strength through artistic isolation.   The es-
sence of our age and of our country as well may also be
sensed as Emily Dickinson speaks through Aaron Copland's
music.   Clarity, simplicity, humor, a keen nose for fakery,
and a deep spiritual commitment--these quintessentially
American traits have been crystallized for all time in the
Twelve Poems of Emily Dickinson.

NOTES

1.   It must, of course, be remembered that Ives's work did
not begin to be recognized until the 1930s.   This group of
composers, therefore, were for a time unaware that they
were following in his footsteps.

2.   See Chapter 24, "The Americanists, " in Chase's Amer-
ica's Music.

3.   Ibid., p. 490.

4.   Douglas Moore, Listening to Music (New York: Norton,
1932).

5. Douglas Moore, From Madrigal to Modern Music (New York: Norton, 1942).

6. Aaron Copland, "Musical Imagination in the Americas, " in Music and Imagination (Cambridge, Massachusetts: Harvard University Press, 1966), p. 94.

7. This quotation appears in Madeline Goss, Modern Music Makers (New York: Dutton, 1952), p. 162.

8. Thomas Scherman, "Douglas Moore, The Optimistic Conservative, " Music Journal, voL 27 (October 1969), p. 25.

9. For a similar characterization of Benét's poetic style see Babette Deutsch, Poetry in Our Time (Garden City, New York: Doubleday, 1963), p. 47.

10. Douglas Moore, "Adam Was My Grandfather" (New York: Galaxy Music, 1938).

11. This song appears in Contemporary Songs in English, edited by Bernard Taylor (New York: Fischer, 1956).

12. Deutsch, p. 200.

13. Waggoner, p. 564.

14. Ibid., p. 568.

15. For an interesting formulation of Roethke's "positive and negative imagery, " see Ralph J. Mills, Jr., Theodore Roethke (Minneapolis: University of Minnesota Press, 1963), p. 42.

16. Waggoner, p. 569.

17. William Grant Still, "My Arkansas Boyhood, " Arkansas Historical Quarterly, (Autumn 1967), pp. 80-81. This article has been reprinted in Robert Bartlett Haas, ed., William Grant Still and the Fusion of Cultures in American Music (Los Angeles: Black Sparrow Press, 1972).

18. William Grant Still, "Winter's Approach" (New York: Schirmer, 1928). This song is currently out of print.

19. Complete Poems of Paul Laurence Dunbar with the In-

troduction to "Lyrics of Lowly Life" by W. D. Howells (New York: Dodd, Mead, 1970), p. x.

20. William Grant Still, "The Breath of a Rose" (New York: Schirmer, 1928).

21. Still, "My Arkansas Boyhood."

22. The Howard Swanson setting of "The Negro Speaks of Rivers" has been published in the recent collection Anthology of Art Songs by Black American Composers (New York: Edward B. Marks Music, 1977).

23. William Grant Still, Songs of Separation (New York: Leeds Music, 1949). This cycle is also out of print. The writer obtained a copy (and of "Winter's Approach") through the kindness of Verna Arvey Still, the composer's widow.

24. Ernst Bacon, Our Musical Idiom (Chicago: Open Court, 1917; reprinted from The Monist, October 1917.)

25. Ernst Bacon, Words on Music (Syracuse, New York: Syracuse University Press, 1960). This is a collection of addresses, essays, and lectures.

26. Ibid., p. 37.

27. Ibid., p. 38.

28. Waggoner, pp. 212-213.

29. Ernst Bacon, "It's all I have to bring" (New York: Schirmer, 1944).

30. Ernst Bacon, "And this of all my hopes" (New York: Schirmer, 1944). These two songs by Bacon appear in the recorded anthology Art Song in America, cited in Chapter II.

31. Waggoner, p. 206.

32. Roy Harris, "Problems of American Composers," in American Composers on American Music, ed. Henry Cowell (Stanford, California: Stanford University Press, 1933), p. 506.

33. Aaron Copland, "Roy Harris" in The New Music, 1900-1906 (New York: Norton, 1968), p. 120.

34. Deutsch, p. 56.

35. This song is published in the Bernard Taylor collection cited in note 11. It also appears in the recording cited in note 30.

36. Copland, The New Music, p. 155.

37. Edward T. Cone, "Conversation with Aaron Copland, " in Perspectives on American Composers (New York: Norton, 1971).

38. Hitchcock, Music in the United States, p. 179.

39. Irving Lowens, from a tribute to Aaron Copland on the occasion of his receiving an honorary degree from Brooklyn College (June 5, 1975). Lowens's and Copland's remarks were reprinted in the newsletter of the Institute for Studies in American Music, vol. V, no. 1 (November 1975).

40. See note 1, Chapter III.

41. Aaron Copland, Twelve Poems of Emily Dickinson (Boosey and Hawkes, 1951). The composer has recorded the complete cycle on the Columbia label with Adele Addison, soprano.

42. Nathan, "The Modern Period--United States of America, " p. 448.

43. Joseph Kerman, "American Music: The Columbia Series (II). " The Hudson Review, vol. 13 (1961), pp. 408 ff.

44. William Flanagan, "American Songs: A Thin Crop, " in Musical America, vol. 72 (February 1952), p. 23.

45. Martha Dickinson Bianchi and Alfred Leete Hampson, eds. , The Poems of Emily Dickinson (Boston: Little, Brown, 1937).

46. The information in the preceding two paragraphs derives from an interview by the author on January 14, 1978, with Carol Mayo, who was at that time professor of voice at Baylor University. Mayo had just been involved in a performance of the full cycle with Copland as accompanist. The concert was given to the Van Cliburn Society in Fort Worth, Texas, on January 12, 1978.

47.   Music Review, vol. 14 (August 1953), p. 249.   The
reviewer is not identified.

48.   Mayo interview.

49.   Ibid.

50.   Ibid.

EPILOGUE

This, then, has been the period of America's "coming of age" in the art song. As a result of our colonial beginnings and our inheritance of the British and other traditions, we initially found it difficult to cast off the "mother country" syndrome. For a long time, we were apologetic, we imported our culture, and we went back to Europe to study in Germany or France. As late as the nineteen twenties, there was still a group of Americans in Paris absorbing French musical and literary influences, but this was to be the last colony of expatriates.

All the while, alongside the European traditions, the new American voice had been struggling to emerge, and again the poetry came first. Poe, one of our earliest literary giants, was the great "nay-sayer" philosophically, to whom evil seemed more inherent and powerful than good. He was obsessed by form, and his masterful structures proved to be a perfect vehicle for Loeffler's over-ripe turn-of-the-century Romanticism.

Emerson, born six years earlier than Poe, brought the new Transcendental note to the century as he proclaimed our connection to a benevolent universe, as well as the uniqueness and importance of the individual. Not only did Emerson have enormous influence on all the great poets who came after him, but he inspired Charles Ives, as well, with the courage to strike out in new directions.

Whitman, following in Emerson's philosophical footsteps, went beyond him in his unconventional use of language.

141

This freedom of form, which seemed to reflect the open expanse of the vast new land, strove to express not only the individual's growing sense of "self" but also his love for his fellow men and women, regardless of color, creed, or social position. Whitman was kindred to Ives also, as he would prove to be to many other American composers of subsequent generations.

Quietly all the while, and unknown to the rest of nineteenth-century America, Emily Dickinson was writing, with her unique genius forging new formal and technical paths, and her meek form concealing a backbone stiffened by Puritan origins. Beginning with Emersonian Transcendence, she moved with suffering to the position that both Life and Death are hard to bear, but nevertheless took up the battle each day, pen in hand. A delay in publication of her works resulted in a lapse of over fifty years before the rich treasure of her poetry became known to American composers. When it did, a flood of settings was the result.

Into the twentieth century, the tide of American lyric poetry continues to flow, and composers continue to find literary counterparts of their own particular view of the American experience. Roy Harris is drawn to Carl Sandburg's plain speech and realistic eye. William Grant Still seeks out Paul Laurence Dunbar and Langston Hughes, who have told us what it feels like to be black in America. Douglas Moore has matched his own lyricism to that of Stephen Vincent Benét and Theodore Roethke.

American song composers of the last hundred years have taken over the musical imagery procedures that became so highly developed in the nineteenth century lied, and have employed them with great impact in setting their own language and poetry. Rhythmic imagery has been derived from combinations of assertive New World speech rhythms, rhythms that were eventually incorporated into ragtime, jazz, spirituals, and other examples of a steady pulse being coupled with a free pulse. [1] Harmonic imagery in the developing American style has often turned to widely spaced, expansive dissonances whose verbal description itself forms a visual image of the nature of the land. Melodic imagery has been as closely tied as rhythmic to the sound patterns and inflections of American speech, and this is reflected in the varyingly smooth and jagged contours of melodic lines.

142

In the art song, as in other forms, the era of "Americanism," which had been such a vital force in the musical history of the United States, declined after 1940, but by then it had served its purpose. American song composers had broken free from their Old World ties and had won the artistic revolution, which lagged well behind the political. In their "coming of age," they had asserted their independence and henceforth would feel free to synthesize any and all influences, whether national, international, or universal, into a personal style.

NOTE

1. Copland, "Musical Imagination...." On page 86 of this lecture, Copland gives an interesting analysis of the way in which the differences between English and American speech rhythms give rise to musical differences in their vocal settings.

143

USERS' NOTE

Out-of-print songs by Charles Loeffler and William Grant
Still discussed in this volume can be obtained from the New
York Public Library's Music Division at Lincoln Center.
The three Griffes songs, now also out-of-print, are in the
music collection of the Library of Congress, in Washington,
D. C.

BIBLIOGRAPHY

A. Bibliographical Tools

Dictionary Catalog of the Music Collection. New York
    Public Library.

Jackson, Richard. United States Music, Sources of Bib-
    liography and Collective Biography. Brooklyn, New
    York: Institute for Studies in American Music, 1976.

Mead, Rita. Doctoral Dissertations in American Music,
    A Classified Bibliography. Brooklyn, New York: In-
    stitute for Studies in American Music, 1974.

Music Index. Annual index to articles on music in vari-
    ous periodicals.

B. American Music

Chase, Gilbert. America's Music. New York: McGraw-
    Hill, 1966.

Hitchcock, H. Wiley. Music in the United States: A
    Historical Introduction. Englewood Cliffs, New Jer-
    sey: Prentice-Hall, 1969.

Howard, John Tasker. Our American Music. New York:
    Crowell, 1965.

Rosenfeld, Paul. An Hour with American Music. Phila-
    delphia: Lippincott, 1929.

145

C. American Art Song

Finck, Henry T. Songs and Song Writers. New York: Scribner's, 1900.

Hall, James Husst. The Art Song. Norman: University of Oklahoma Press, 1953.

Nathan, Hans. "The Modern Period--United States of America, " in A History of Song, ed. Denis Stevens. New York: Norton, 1960.

Upton, Wm. Treat. Art Song in America. New York: Ditson, 1930 (Johnson Reprint Corp., 1969).

Yerbury, Grace D. Song in America from Early Times to About 1850. Metuchen, New Jersey: Scarecrow Press, 1971.

D. Composers

Anderson, Donna K. The Works of Charles T. Griffes: A Descriptive Catalogue. Dissertation, Ann Arbor, 1966.

_____. The Works of Charles T. Griffes: An Annotated Bibliography-Discography. Boulder, Colorado: College Music Society, 1977.

Anderson, E. Ruth (comp.). Contemporary American Composers, A Biographical Dictionary. Boston: G. K. Hall, 1976.

Bacon, Ernst. Words on Music. Westport, Connecticut: Greenwood Press, 1973 (originally published by Syracuse University Press, 1960).

Bauer, Marion. "Charles Griffes as I Remember Him, " Musical Quarterly, vol. 29 (July 1943), pp. 355-380.

Bellaman, Henry. "Charles Ives: The Man and His Music, " Musical Quarterly, vol. 19, no. 1 (January 1933), pp. 45-58.

Block, Maxine (ed.). Current Biography. New York: H. W. Wilson, 1940-

Boretz, Benjamin, and Cone, Edward (eds.). Perspectives on American Composers. New York: Norton, 1971.

Carter, Elliott. "Ives Today: His Vision and Challenge," Musical Quarterly, vol. 21, no. 4 (May-June 1944), pp. 199-202.

Chase, Gilbert (ed.). The American Composer Speaks. Baton Rouge, Louisiana: State University Press, 1966.

Copland, Aaron. The New Music. New York: Norton, 1968.

_____. Music and the Imagination. Cambridge, Massachusetts: Harvard University Press, 1966.

Cowell, Henry and Sidney. Charles Ives and His Music. New York: Oxford University Press, 1969.

Engel, Carl. "Charles Martin Loeffler," Musical Quarterly, vol. 2, no. 3 (July 1925), pp. 320 ff.

Flanagan, William. "American Songs: A Thin Crop," Musical America, vol. 72 (February 1952), pp. 23 ff.

Gilman, Lawrence. Edward MacDowell, A Study. New York: DaCapo Press Reprint Series, 1969.

Goss, Madeleine. Modern Music Makers. New York: Dutton, 1952.

Haas, Robert Bartlett (ed.). William Grant Still and the Fusion of Cultures in American Music. Los Angeles: Black Sparrow Press, 1972.

Harris, Roy, et al. The Bases of Artistic Creation. New Brunswick, New Jersey: Rutgers University Press, 1942.

Hill, Edwin Burlingame. "Charles Martin Loeffler," Modern Music, vol. 13, no. 1 (November-December 1935), pp. 26-31.

Hitchcock, H. Wiley. Ives. New York: Oxford University Press, 1977.

147

Ives, Charles. "Essays Before a Sonata." Reprinted in Three Classics in the Aesthetic of Music. New York: Dover, 1962.

Kerman, Joseph. "American Music: The Columbia Series (II)." The Hudson Review, vol. 13 (1961), pp. 408 ff.

Kirkpatrick, John. Charles E. Ives--Memos. New York: Norton, 1972.

Livingston, Carolyn Lambeth. The Songs of Charles T. Griffes. Master's Thesis, Department of Music, University of North Carolina, 1947.

MacDowell, Edward. Critical and Historical Essays (ed. W. J. Baltzell). Boston: Stanhope, 1912.

Maisel, Edward M. Charles T. Griffes. New York: Knopf, 1943.

Mason, Daniel Gregory. Contemporary Composers. New York: Macmillan, 1918.

Perlis, Vivian. Charles Ives Remembered (an Oral History). New Haven, Connecticut: Yale University Press, 1974.

Perry, Rosalie Sandra. Charles Ives and the American Mind. Kent, Ohio: Kent State University Press, 1974.

Rorem, Ned. Music from Inside Out. New York: Braziller, 1967.

Scherman, Thomas. "Douglas Moore, The Optimistic Conservative," Music Journal, vol. 27 (October 1969), pp. 24-25.

Slonimsky, Nicholas (comp.). Baker's Biographical Dictionary of Musicians. New York: Schirmer, 1978.

E.   Poets and Poetry

Aldrich, Thomas Bailey. The Poems, Volume I. Boston and New York: Houghton Mifflin, 1930.

Allen, Gay Wilson. American Prosody. Atlanta: American Book Co., 1935.

_____. Carl Sandburg. Minneapolis: University of Minnesota Press, 1972.

Anderson, Charles R. (ed.). Sidney Lanier, Poems and Poem Outlines. Baltimore: Johns Hopkins Press, 1945.

Atkinson, Brooks (ed.). The Writings of Ralph Waldo Emerson. New York: Modern Library, 1940.

Benét, Stephen Vincent. Selected Works. New York: Farrar and Rinehart, 1942.

Bianchi, Martha Dickinson, and Hampson, Alfred Leete (eds.). The Poems of Emily Dickinson. Boston: Little, Brown, 1937.

Bontemps, Arna (ed.). American Negro Poetry. New York: Hill and Wang, 1963.

Cooper, James Fenimore, Jr. Afterglow. New Haven, Connecticut: Yale University Press, 1918.

Cullen, Countee. On These I Stand (An Anthology of the Best Poems). New York: Harper and Row, 1947.

Deutsch, Babette. Poetry in Our Time. Garden City, New York: Doubleday (Anchor Books), 1963.

Dunbar, Paul Laurence. Complete Poems with the Introduction to "Lyrics of Lowly Life" by W. D. Howells. New York: Dodd, Mead, 1970.

Eliot, T. S. The Music of Poetry. Glasgow: Jackson, Son and Co., 1942.

Emerson, Ralph Waldo. Poems. Cambridge, Massachusetts: Riverside Press, 1895.

Fussell, Paul, Jr. Poetic Meter and Poetic Form. New York: Random House, 1967.

Hart, James D. The Oxford Companion to American Literature. New York: Oxford University Press, 1948.

149

Herschberg, Max J.   The Reader's Encyclopedia of American Literature.   New York: Crowell, 1962.

Holmes, Oliver Wendell.   The Complete Poetical Works. Boston and New York: Houghton, Mifflin, 1895.

Howells, William Dean.   Poems.   Boston: Ticknor, 1886.

Hughes, Langston.   Collected Poems.   New York: Knopf, 1969.

Johnson, Thomas H.   (ed.).   The Complete Poems of Emily Dickinson.   Boston: Little, Brown, 1960.

Kunitz, Stanley, and Haycraft, Howard.   American Authors 1600-1900.   New York: H. W. Wilson, 1960.

Lanier, Sidney.   The Science of English Verse.   New York: Scribner's, 1893.

Lawson, Victor.   Dunbar Critically Examined.   Washington, D. C.:   Associated Publishers, 1941.

Lindsay, Nicholas Vachel.   Collected Poems.   New York: Macmillan, 1925.

Longfellow, Henry Wadsworth.   Poems, Volume III. Boston and New York: Houghton, Mifflin, 1910.

Perry, Margaret.   A Bio-Bibliography of Countee P. Cullen.   Westport, Connecticut: Greenwood, 1971.

Sandburg, Carl.   Chicago Poems.   New York: Holt, 1916.

Spiller, Robert E.; Thorpe, Willard; Johnson, Thomas J.; Canby, Henry Seidel; and Ludwig, Richard M. (eds.).   Literary History of the United States.   New York: Macmillan, 1963.

Sprague, Charles.   The Poetical and Prose Writings. Boston: A. Williams, 1876.

Tabb, John Bannister.   The Poetry of Father Tabb (ed. Francis A. Litz).   New York: Dodd, Mead, 1928.

Thoreau, Henry David. Walden. New York: Harper and Row, 1965.

Untermeyer, Louis. "The Swimmers," The Yale Review, vol. 4, no. 4 (July 1915), pp. 786-787.

Valéry, Paul. The Art of Poetry. New York: Vintage, 1961.

Waggoner, Hyatt H. American Poets from the Puritans to the Present. New York: Dell, 1968.

Whitman, Walt. Leaves of Grass, The First (1855) Edition (ed. Malcolm Cowley). New York: Viking Press, 1960.

Whittier, John Greenleaf. The Complete Poetical Works. Boston: Houghton, Mifflin, 1894.

Wiggin, Kate Douglas, and Smith, Nora Archibald (eds.). Golden Numbers. New York: Doubleday, Doran, 1902.

F. Poetry and Music

Brown, Calvin S. Music and Literature. Athens: University of Georgia Press, 1948.

Castelnuovo-Tedesco, Mario. "Music and Poetry: Problems of a Songwriter," in The Musical Quarterly, vol. 30, no. 1 (1944), pp. 102-111.

Cooke, Deryck. The Language of Music. London: Oxford University Press, 1959.

Eliot, T. S. The Music of Poetry. Glasgow: Jackson, Son and Co., 1942.

Ferguson, Donald. Music as Metaphor. Minneapolis: University of Minnesota Press, 1960.

Ivey, Donald. Song: Anatomy, Imagery and Styles. New York: Free Press, 1970.

Langer, Susanne K. Feeling and Form. New York: Scribner's, 1953.

_____ (ed.). Reflections on Art. Baltimore: Johns Hopkins Press, 1958.

Perrins, Laurence. Literature--Structure, Sound and Sense. New York: Harcourt, Brace and World, 1970.

APPENDIX I: INDEX OF SONGS CITED

153

APPENDIX II: INDEX OF SONGS BY COMPOSERS

157

163